Canyon Country

MOUNTAIN BIKING

by
F. A. Barnes and Tom Kuehne

A complete illustrated guide to
mountain biking
in the unique canyon country
of southeastern Utah

Another Canyon Country Guidebook
1988

This book is the SEVENTEENTH in a series of practical guides to travel and recreation in the scenic Canyon Country region of the Four Corners States

All written material is by
F. A. Barnes and Tom Kuehne

Photographs and maps are by F. A. Barnes unless otherwise credited

Sketches are by
Kathy Nunley
and F. A. Barnes

CONTENTS

CONTENTS CONTINUED ON NEXT PAGE

FOREWORD

Welcome to southeastern Utah's canyon country, the mountain-biking mecca. No matter where else you may have been biking, you will find new and challenging trails and experiences in canyon country. It's different -- like nowhere else. How?

It's the geology. For megayears, unrelenting erosion has sculpted a high-desert sandstone basin into a veritable maze of redrock canyons, soaring plateaus, slickrock domes and fins, vast rock escarpments and lofty mountains, whose bases are slashed by still more canyons.

Where else can you mountain-bike one day in the shadowed depths or along the rims of sheer-walled sandstone gorges a thousand feet deep, then the next day travel aspen-bordered trails, both from the same base camp?

Where else can you find literally hundreds of miles of uncrowded trails -- trails so remote and seldom traveled by anyone that, on them, "gridlock" is defined as seeing anyone else at all on the same trail?

Where else can you bike for endless miles along challenging routes on solid slickrock "dunes," with spectacular scenery and unique beauty in every direction?

Where else can you find yourself being welcomed as warmly as in canyon country, where there are so many trails within range of one base that you don't have to compete with runners, day-hikers, backpackers or horses for fascinating trails of all kinds?

Canyon country is different -- like nowhere else in the world. Once you learn what enormous variety this region has to offer, in both trails and scenery, you'll be spoiled for anywhere else.

Enjoy!

F. A. Barnes, co-author, editor and publisher

BASIC INFORMATION

GUIDEBOOK SERIES

This is one of a series of practical *Canyon Country* guide books, each one covering some aspect of the canyon country of southeastern Utah. In addition to this book and others that describe the various kinds of scenic access roads and backcountry trails in the region -- trails for hiking, biking and other recreational vehicles -- there are books that describe the region's spectacular geology, its prehistory, and its human and natural history. There are also *Canyon Country* maps that cover the entire region described in the various road and trail books.

Some of these books and maps are mentioned by title at appropriate places in this book, and all are listed in the FURTHER READING section at the end of the book.

AREAS COVERED

The canyon country region covered by this book is shaded on the map on the inside-front cover.

For practical purposes, this region has been divided into geographically distinct areas, as shown on the same map. As an aid to access, navigation and guidance, the roads and backcountry trails described throughout this book are listed as being in one or another of these areas.

ACCESS ROADS

Paved and numbered federal and state highways define some of the perimeters of the six areas covered by this book, providing easy access to each. Interstate 70 borders the Island and Arches areas. Utah 24 and 95 allow access to the Maze area. U.S.191 borders the Arches, Island, La Sals and Canyon Rims areas. Utah 46 provides access to the La Sals area from the south. Utah 211 provides access to the Needles and Canyon Rims areas.

Other paved, graveled and graded dirt roads provide further access within each of these areas. Some serve primarily as access to the trail segments and loops described in this book. Others are worthy bike trails in themselves.

Access road names used are those on the *Canyon Country* maps listed under individual trail descriptions.

The gravel and dirt access roads described are usually passable to 2-wheel-drive highway vehicles, but may have local bad spots or may be in generally bad condition due to recent precipitation, heavy mineral exploration traffic, lack of maintenance, or some combination of these factors.

The various access roads are described by area in the trail descriptions chapter.

REGIONAL TERRAIN

The terrain in the region covered by this book varies drastically, even within each of the six defined areas. The terrain in each of the six areas is described by area in the trail descriptions chapter.

7

NAVIGATION

Off-highway navigation in canyon country is seldom simple.
Several factors combine to make maps and map-reading skills
essential and, even then, easy trail-finding is not always
assured. Some of the factors that complicate navigation are
natural, but the worst are human in origin.

The two principal natural factors are terrain that in some
areas lacks features prominent enough to appear on topographic
maps, and stretches of sand and slickrock that show few permanent
traces of the trails that cross them.

There are four clues to watch for when crossing expanses of
slickrock on which the trail being followed may be obscure.
These are: wheel tracks visible in patches of sand or pothole
sediments, small ledges of sandstone crumpled by wheels, and
bulldozer tracks. These may not be found on all trails. If
these clues are not enough, scout the edges of the slickrock mass
for indications of where the trail leaves it and continues.

Of the human factors, one is the lack of directional and
name signs. A few of the trail and road junctions in the area
covered by this book are marked by signs, but most are not.

The greatest single problem to navigation, however, is
mineral search activity that obscures or realigns established
trails, creates new trails, or laces huge areas with parallel and
intersecting trails in support of seismographic surveys. Such
operations can, within a few days, turn a huge, unspoiled natural
area that was penetrated by a single obscure trail or none, into
a veritable maze of bulldozed, eroding trails that destroy the
natural beauty and either end at a drill site or go nowhere.

Since existing laws governing the search for minerals on
public land do not prevent such abusive activities, those who
intend to travel canyon country backcountry trails must be
prepared for the resulting navigational problems.

The trails described in this book have all been traveled personally by one or both of its authors, but as long as the mineral industry has the right to change existing trails and create new ones, there can be no assurance that any trail description will remain valid indefinitely.

Because of the noted natural and human factors, optimum trail navigation in much of canyon country consists of the skillful use of maps and the verbal descriptions in this and other books, plus trail-reading abilities, persistence and, in some cases, an element of luck. Only a few of the trails described in this are so well defined, and so protected by the surrounding terrain, that they can be followed without the use of navigational skills, and most of these are within Canyonlands National Park.

On most of the trails described in detail in this book, there is little chance of getting lost, although on a few it is possible to become confused at the many trail junctions. Although some of the numerous spurs off of some trails are worth exploring, they can also confuse navigation.

Of course, if all else fails, and you find yourself hopelessly confused about where you are in some isolated area of canyon country, you can always fall back on the philosophy Walt Kelly had one of his characters express:

"How can you be lost if you don't care where you are?"

LAND OWNERSHIP

Southeastern Utah's canyon country is unique in that more than 90% of the land is owned by either the state or federal government, with administration assigned to the several agencies involved. The remainder of the land is privately owned.

The administration of state land is under various state agencies, such as the Division of Parks & Recreation and the State Land Board. The administration of federal land is under various federal agencies, such as the National Park Service, the U.S. Forest Service, the Bureau of Land Management, and the Bureau of Indian Affairs.

Each of these state and federal agencies has its own distinct policies and regulations concerning the use of the public land under its administration. Basically, bikers and others who wish to use public lands, whether state or federal, are free to do so unless the land is otherwise posted. This is presently rare within the canyon country region.

Those who want more information about land-use policies will find them summarized in another book in the *Canyon Country* series titled *Canyon Country* EXPLORING. This book also provides details about access to the several types of public land and waterways in the region, as well as policies concerning flight over them, and gives a brief summary of the region's history.

As with anywhere else, access to private land in canyon country is only with the owner's prior permission. The one exception to this is where established public roads pass through private land, as along the slopes of the La Sal Mountains. In such places, public passage is permitted as long as travelers stay strictly on the roads and close all gates encountered.

Generally, the rare private land in the region is fenced and posted. The existence of a fence alone, however, does not in itself mean private land, because most BLM and USFS land is divided by fences into grazing allotments. Thus, bikers who encounter unposted fences or gates, may feel free to continue along the road or trail, but should leave all gates as found, either open or closed.

FOOT TRAILS

There are very few established and marked hiking trails in canyon country. Most of those that do exist are in parks and monuments, or follow routes that are hazardous for mountain bikes. The policies of both federal and state parks and monuments limit the use of established hiking trails within their borders to foot traffic. Wheeled vehicles are prohibited, other than wheel chairs on a few paved trails. On BLM and USFS lands the policy is similar.

However, unlike other places, where the few public trails must be shared by a variety of users, in canyon country there is no need for conflict among users. The authors of this book thus recommend that the relatively few established hiking trails in the region be avoided by bikers, because there are more than enough other challenging trails and routes.

Hiking trail in Arches National Park

BASE CAMPS

Overnight facilities within canyon country that can serve as base camps for mountain biking range from the motels and commercial campgrounds found in its developed communities, to developed public campgrounds scattered around the region, to primitive backcountry camping. Except within national and state parks, and on a few posted parcels of private land, primitive camping is permitted anywhere within the region covered by this book. The following area-by-area summary provides more details.

Trails in the Arches and La Sals areas can be explored from a variety of base camps. There are motels and commercial campgrounds in and near Moab, and developed public campgrounds in Arches National Park and the La Sal Mountains. There are no traveler amenities within these areas other than limited supplies and automotive services at the nearby communities of Thompson, Gateway, Paradox, Bedrock, La Sal, and Crescent Junction.

Trails in the Canyon Rims and Needles areas can also be explored from a variety of base camps. There are motels and commercial campgrounds in and near Moab and Monticello, and a campground at the commercial resort near the entrance to the Needles District of Canyonlands National Park. There are developed public campgrounds within Canyonlands N. P., Canyon Rims Recreation Area and Newspaper Rock State Park. There are no traveler amenities within these areas other than at Moab and Monticello, although automotive fuel and limited camping supplies are available at the commercial resort near the park entrance.

Island Area trails can also be explored from a variety of base camps. There are motels and commercial campgrounds in and near Moab, and developed public campgrounds at Dead Horse Point State Park and the Green River Overlook on the Island-in-the-Sky. There are also primitive campsites at designated places along the White Rim Trail and its spurs. Because of very limited access from Interstate 70 and the northern 15 miles of U.S.191, the town of Green River does not make a suitable base for exploring trails within the Island Area.

Maze Area trails can be explored from the town of Green River or from the developed state park campground at Goblin Valley, but both bases require considerable highway and dirt road travel before the trails are reached. The most practical way to bike Maze area trails is from a primitive camp within more convenient range, such as near the Hans Flat access road, in the general vicinity of the Hans Flat ranger station. Rangers there can suggest suitable sites, and provide current information about primitive campsites along the trails within Canyonlands National Park and the adjacent Glen Canyon National Recreation Area.

WATER

Most natural water sources in canyon country have long since been permanently contaminated by grazing domestic livestock, which carry and spread giardiasis and other infectious diseases to which humans are susceptible.

Thus, all surface water is suspect -- including that in rivers, streams, lakes and ponds of all sizes -- and should not be used for drinking or cooking without proper treatment. Some commercial chemical treatment systems are suitable, if followed with appropriate filtration. Biologically contaminated water can also be made potable, if not palatable, by at least five minutes of vigorous boiling, longer in higher elevations.

The only native water in canyon country that is safe to drink untreated is from dripping springs, where the water has not yet come in contact with the ground. There are many such springs, but few deliver enough water for practical purposes.

The most practical approach to the problem of water in this arid high-desert region is to carry along all that will be needed for the length of trip planned, even though this may not always be convenient. Giardiasis and other such intestinal infections are not convenient either.

On longer, several-day bike trips, it may be necessary to provide support from a motorized vehicle that can carry all the potable water needed, or to take along the means for purifying the native water found along the way. Within the region's parks, rangers can indicate where water is available along authorized routes, but the water should still be considered suspect.

Perennial spring, Cane Creek Canyon

SUPPLIES

The only major sources for various supplies within or near the region covered by this book are the towns of Moab, Monticello and Green River. Limited supplies may be available at the small settlements of La Sal, Paradox, Gateway, Bedrock, Crescent Junction and Thompson, and at the commercial resort near the entrance to the Needles district of Canyonlands National Park.

Bikers who plan to travel backcountry trails must take along everything they will need for the entire trip. The only practical alternatives to this are to travel with a motorized support vehicle, or arrange to meet one at a specific place along the route.

SERVICES

The only sources for various traveler services within or near the region covered by this book are the towns of Moab, Monticello and Green River, although the usual emergency automotive services are available along the main highways.

On backcountry roads and trails, the only practical courses are to be prepared for self-help, or take along a motorized support vehicle. Groups of bikers also have the option of sending someone back or ahead for any necessary help, should mechanical or health problems arise.

Even so, for bikers who are planning to take any of the longer trails, especially those that require more than one day to travel, a small but powerful CB radio can provide a margin of safety. While these may not be able to reach very far during daylight hours, especially from within deep canyons, their effective range increases enough at night to reach the posts that monitor the CB emergency bands. There are several search-and-rescue organizations in the region.

HEALTH PRECAUTIONS

Most bikers are aware of what is necessary to stay healthy and comfortable under varying conditions. This involves the wearing of layered clothing in cooler weather, and wearing a hat and loose-fitting, light-colored clothing when it is warm.

In canyon country, daytime temperatures can exceed 90 degrees. For active bikers, this, coupled with the region's elevation and low relative humidity, creates a risk of serious dehydration and heat exhaustion. Unlike other areas, in the desert it is possible to start a trail at a high elevation, enjoy a long and relatively easy ride, but still lose considerable body water, with no assured replacement beyond what is carried.

Dehydration can affect mental alertness and physical coordination, either of which can affect safety. As a normal precaution, two large water bottles should be carried. For longer rides, or during hot weather, even more water is advisable.

The conscious perception of thirst is not a reliable first indication of dehydration. A considerable amount of water can be lost before it becomes apparent. Thus, while biking in canyon country, even in the cooler seasons, it is advisable to drink water at regular intervals. Failing to do this creates a risk of electrolytic imbalance with the attendant bodily discomfort and possible malfunction.

PREHISTORIC REMNANTS

The canyon country of southeastern Utah was once occupied by two distinct cultures of prehistoric Indians, the Fremonts and the Anasazis. Remnants of these cultures -- ruins, rock art and other artifacts -- are found throughout the region, and are one of its major attractions.

However, all such remains of these former inhabitants are protected by both state and federal laws. It is illegal to collect or in any way disturb antiquities on public land. They can be studied and photographed, but should be left as found, for the enjoyment of others and for study by scientists.

Bikers who might want to know more about this region's prehistoric cultures will find two other *Canyon Country* series books useful. *Canyon Country* PREHISTORIC INDIANS describes the two cultures in detail, while *Canyon Country* PREHISTORIC ROCK ART provides a comprehensive look at this region's prehistoric pictographs and petroglyphs. Both books are well illustrated.

SEASONS AND WEATHER

SEASONS

Because of the high-desert climate that prevails throughout the non-mountainous areas of canyon country, the best seasons for exploring its trails are spring, March through May, and fall, September through November. Biking is, of course, possible during the summer, even though daytime temperatures in the lowlands are generally in the 90's. The higher elevations are cooler. Most of this area can also be biked during normal winters, although even light snow may make the steeper stretches of some trails difficult.

From November through May, motor vehicle roads and trails in the La Sal and Abajo mountains are generally closed by snow above the 6,000-foot level, but are normally open from June through October. Mountain bikers planning trips on any of the various mountain trails in early spring or late fall should first check trail conditions at the U.S. Forest Service offices in either Moab or Monticello.

WEATHER

The weather in canyon country is generally moderate and predictable, with sunny, clear days dominating most of the year. The exceptions, however, can be uncomfortable to mountain bikers on trails or in backcountry campsites.

Winter weather is predominantly sunny and calm between the occasional storms. Daytime temperatures varying with elevation in the 30 to 50 degrees range, with nights from 15 to 30 degrees. Spring and fall daytime temperatures range from 40 to 70 degrees, again depending on elevation, while nights are correspondingly cooler.

In the spring, however, the changing season often brings rain, overcast and wind, although these seldom last longer than two or three days. Between such passing storms, calm, sunny days dominate. Early spring, March through April, is the most variable and unpredictable. This improves in late spring.

Early summer is generally warm and dry, with only occasional winds. During mid to late summer, local thunderhead cloud systems build over the mountains and other highlands. These offer respite from the summer sun, but also spread broad paths of moderate to severe thunder showers and attendant winds as they drift across the region.

These localized weather systems become less frequent as fall approaches. From early September through November, the weather is generally dry, windless and sunny, although the changing season usually brings at least one major storm system through the region in late October. Such storms deposit the season's first snow in the higher elevations. After that, canyon country enjoys a long Indian Summer that often lasts well into December.

PARKING

Whatever trails are to be traveled, bikers will need to park their access vehicles beside main highways or in backcountry locations that are often remote from any signs of civilization.

For the most part, it is legal to park vehicles almost anywhere on public land, off of the highway right-of-way. The exceptions to this are in established state and federal parks and monuments, where vehicle parking may be restricted or limited.

To date, there have been very few problems in the region with theft or vandalism of vehicles. There are, however, other potential problems that should be considered. For example, it may not be safe to park where rockfalls are likely to occur, where the region's occasional rain storms might cause flooding, or where such flooding might cut off egress to a paved road.

Further, during the warmer months, April through October, precautions should be taken to minimize adverse effects on heat-sensitive items left in a vehicle. It is also advisable to lock vehicles, and either take along expensive valuables or leave them out of sight within the vehicle.

If these practical precautions are taken, bikers should find few if any problems with parking almost anywhere in canyon country.

BACKCOUNTRY ETHICS

Most mountain bikers have, of course, long since developed their own codes of behavior toward other users of the trails they travel elsewhere, but canyon country trails present novel conditions and circumstances that ethical bikers might wish to consider.

THE LAND

First, the land itself deserves some kind of special consideration. This region was the last to be explored in the contiguous United States. Its very broken, high-desert nature left most of it undesirable for homesteading, and the sparse minerals it contained left very few patented mineral claims.

Thus, until about the 1940s, most of the region was "wasteland," unwanted by anyone, used only by ranchers for the grazing of domestic livestock, with even that use marginal and destructive to the region's delicate high-desert ecosystems.

Then, urgent national needs for uranium, vanadium and petroleum products brought cycles of prospecting, mining, and drilling to the region, and these activities created most of the present network of backcountry roads and trails. At present, such activities are at low ebb, and recreational users of the trails can enjoy them without fear of conflict with industrial users. That has not always been the case.

Despite the massive damage done to this region's spectacular natural beauty by the mineral industry, ethical recreational users have adopted a policy of inflicting minimal additional damage on the land by exploring, mapping, and naming the better existing backcountry trails, by staying on these trails with all vehicles, and by leaving the land uncluttered. The authors of this book hope that mountain bikers will adopt this same backcountry ethic.

OTHER USERS

In spite of the fact that most of the region's backcountry trails see very little vehicular use of any kind, mountain bikers will occasionally encounter motorized vehicles, especially on weekends and holidays, and in the region's two national parks. Since such encounters are rare otherwise, and will probably continue to be, there is no reason for conflict between motorized and non-motorized users of the endless miles of backcountry public roads and trails in the region.

While there will no doubt be exceptions, human nature being what it is, for the most part off-road vehicle users deserve the same kind of consideration and ethical interface that mountain bikers offer each other.

In many cases, bikers unaccustomed to the rigors of the land and its arid climate will personally benefit from the creation of a polite and ethical interface with motorized users, who will almost always be happy to share their water or tools with bikers who have underestimated distances, or who have had mechanical problems due to the rugged terrain.

Thus, the authors of this book suggest that a polite, friendly interface with other trail users is the most civilized approach, especially since the majority of them will be local residents out for much the same purposes -- to revel in the skillful use of their special vehicles while, at the same time, enjoying the beauty and novelty of the land itself.

BACKCOUNTRY HAZARDS

As with backcountry navigation, the hazards that may be encountered by mountain bikers in the canyon country hinterlands fall into two categories, natural and manmade. While all such hazards can be avoided by simply staying on the mapped and recommended trails, most bikers will want to supplement this sport with primitive camping and a certain amount of backcountry exploring on foot, and should thus be aware of these hazards.

The manmade hazards are largely the remnants of past mineral search and development activities such as open mine shafts, bulldozing that has left unstable slopes, and abandoned equipment and structures. Since almost all such mines shafts were made in the search for uranium, they are exceptionally hazardous. In addition to the obvious dangers from rockfall or collapse, such mines are almost always contaminated with dangerous quantities of radioactive particles and radon gas. Even nearby structures may be contaminated with these subtle hazards to health and longevity. It is thus strongly recommended that all mining areas be avoided.

The only other manmade hazards apt to be encountered by bikers are the ubiquitous range cattle. Whenever possible, these should also be avoided, since their sheer size alone makes them dangerous, and the bulls may be aggressive. Cattle-control fences and gates can also be dangerous if not seen in time.

Most of the natural geologic hazards in canyon country are obvious, such as its cliffs and other rugged terrain, but mountain bikers unaccustomed to such predominantly vertical terrain should take special care to be wary of sheer drops, especially those with crumbling edges.

In certain seasons, the threat of flash flooding should not be taken lightly, especially near water courses in canyon bottoms. Even normally arid drainages can fill with raging torrents of water in minutes during heavy rain, rain that might have fallen miles away. Backcountry campers should pick their sites carefully, especially during inclement weather, seasonal storms or the summer thundershower season.

There are only three wildlife species that can be hazardous to backcountry bikers. Rattlesnakes and scorpions are relatively scarce, and nocturnal during the warmer months, so will rarely be seen. The more common garter snakes and bull-snakes are quite harmless. Black widow spiders are also fairly common, but are so reclusive that they are rarely spotted. Only their patternless webs will be noticed, coming from under boulders or from small, protected alcoves along the bases of sandstone cliffs.

Only two kinds of rattlesnakes range within canyon country, both of them sub-species of the Western Rattlesnake, *Crotalus viridis.* One sub-species, the Hopi Rattler, *Crotalus viridis nuntius,* is slowly spreading into canyon country from its former very limited range in northern Arizona. This snake is quite small, usually less that two feet long, and is mostly nocturnal. Its markings are clean and distinct.

The sub-species that already occupies the region is the Midget Faded Rattler, *Crotalus viridis concolor.* This little snake's name reflects its appearance. It rarely exceeds two feet in length, and its overall color is beige, sometimes tinged with red, with its indistinct markings quite faded-looking. Since it is rare in addition to being largely nocturnal, it is seldom seen, but hikers should be wary while walking or climbing where visibility is limited, such as through brush or up rocky ledges.

Although these two tiny reptiles are quite venomous, both are shy and retiring by nature. They are thus not as hazardous as rattlesnake species in other parts of the country. During the cooler months, when the nights are too cold for much insect and reptile activity, many high desert wildlife species revert to diurnal behavior patterns, and are thus seen more often, hunting or foraging during the daylight hours. This is also true of certain predatory mammals, who adapt to the changing habits of their prey.

Scorpions are not common in canyon country, although they are spotted occasionally. They are not the highly venomous species found in other regions of the southwest. While the fairly common black widow spider is quite venomous, this species is also quite shy and thus poses no real danger.

Experienced canyon country campers know that during the warmer months this high desert's wildlife is more active at night. As a precaution, they generally choose to sleep on large, flat-topped boulders, where small nocturnal animals are less apt to go, or in tents with integral floors and zippered entryways.

As in all natural environments, this region's snakes, insects and other creatures are part of the overall ecosystem. While the more dangerous species should be avoided, they should not be killed or disturbed. Backcountry ethical standards require that native creatures be left to live their relatively short lives in peace.

Midget Faded Rattlesnake

SPECIAL EQUIPMENT

Rocks and sand are a part of mountain biking in the desert. They also emphasize some equipment needs. Sand can penetrate almost anything. Sealed wheel-hubs are more important here than elsewhere. Sand can also cause seizing in chain links. The best prevention is to keep the chain clean of excessive lubricant, then clean and relubricate it after each major use.

Equipment should include two water-bottle cages per bike, a spare tube and tool kit per group, and tire liners. Besides rim-pinch flats, most flats follow encounters with cactus spines or sharp twigs. In some developed areas, low-growing plants called "goatheads" have sharp-pointed seed-pods that are hazardous to feet and bike tires.

A portage strap is seldom needed in canyon country. It is possible to ride all of the ATB trails here, with only minimal portaging over short stretches. Even in slickrock areas without established trails, it is rarely necessary to carry or lift a bike more than a few feet. Headlights are also unnecessary. Very few canyon country trails are suitable for night-riding.

19

Many bikers have heard little about Utah's canyon country except the Moab Slickrock Bike Trail, and wonder about "slicks." Such tires do provide the best traction on slickrock. However, the Slickrock Bike Trail is unique. Although there are many other trail-less expanses of slickrock on which to bike, the other trails described in this book offer terrain whose chief delight is variety -- packed sand, packed rubble, deep wash sand, and domes, folds and fins of sandstone of various types and textures. Thus, normal mountain biking tires are quite suitable for canyon country, although lower tire pressure, to increase traction, is recommended for the Slickrock Bike Trail and on other trail-less routes dominated by bare sandstone.

Cyclometers are becoming increasingly popular on mountain bikes, as more and more bikers combine trail riding with extended touring. They can be very useful for navigating canyon country trails. Obsessive attention to a cyclometer, however, can interfere with an otherwise delightful ride. Thus, as with some of the other equipment items mentioned above, cyclometers are more a matter of personal preference than vital need.

Moab Slickrock Bike Trail

TRAIL DESCRIPTION FORMAT

TRAIL NAME

Where trail names are in popular use, or have appeared in print, these are used. For trails with no name history, names were assigned. These were chosen from named geographic features near the trail. Most of the trail names used do not appear on U.S.G.S. topographic maps or on state road maps, but they do appear on commercial maps available within the region.

TRAIL SUMMARY

In this section, a brief summary is given of the trail's scenic highlights, special points of interest and other general information, as an aid to trail selection.

TRAIL TYPE

As an aid to those who use this book, trail segments are classified into three types: "spur," "connecting" and "loop." A "spur" trail is a dead-end trail that has no practical connections with other named trails anywhere near its end. A "connecting" trail is one that connects two or more access roads or named trails. A "loop" trail is one that, as described, begins and ends from the same access road or other trail. A loop trail may have spurs, and may be joined by a connecting trail, but is still a distinct stretch of trail that is worth traveling as a loop.

LAND OWNERSHIP

As noted earlier, there is little private property in canyon country, but the administration of the public land is divided among several federal and state agencies. Where a particular trail passes through areas with significantly differing usage policies, that is noted in the trail description section.

MAPS

With each trail described, the title of the commercial map that shows that trail, as well as other nearby trails and access roads, is listed in this section. Even with these maps, however, bikers will soon discover that navigation skills are also essential to getting around in canyon country. As the old saying goes -- "the map is not the territory."

MILEAGES

Approximate mileages are given for each trail segment. For spur trails, the round trip distance is given. If a spur trail has other worthwhile spurs, one-way mileages for these appear in the trail description. For connecting trails, the one-way distance is given. For loop trails, the one-way distance back to the point of origin is given, exclusive of any spurs along the loop. One-way mileages for such spurs generally appear in the trail description.

TIME REQUIRED

This section indicates how long it will take an intermediate biker, in only average physical condition, to compete the trail comfortably. A strong biker, or one in a hurry, can reduce the indicated times by about 20%. Since all of the described trails are two-track, the time required to complete some of them can be reduced by driving part of the way. The trails on which this is most feasible are identified in the ACCESS section.

Many spur trails are also interesting. Such spurs are identified in the trail description, but exploring them adds to the total time required to complete the trail being described.

BEST SEASON

This section notes the best seasons for the trail being described, and lists any problems that might occur while trying to bike it in other seasons.

DIFFICULTY

This section summarizes the amount of work involved in completing the trail. An experienced rider will still find any trail easier than an inexperienced biker and, other factors being equal, will burn fewer calories on the same trail. In this section the following factors are identified and taken into account: trail gradients, elevation changes, both net and within the route, and the percentages of wash sand, drift sand, rubble, bare slickrock and other trail hazards. The difficulty rating applies only if the trail is taken as described. Taking a trail in the direction opposite to the described route will usually change the difficulty rating.

The difficulty ratings used in the trail descriptions are: easy, easy/moderate, moderate, moderate/strenuous, and strenuous.

TECHNICAL RATING

This section will indicate the extent to which a moderately skilled rider can expect to dismount or touch the trail along the route, and therefore the degree to which the trail demands a proper line, or special technique, or both. On an "easy" trail, neither the line nor technique is much of a factor, while they both are on a "moderate" trail. The standard for the "technical" rating is the Moab Slickrock Bike Trail. Some trails offer convenient options for exciting, technical riding literally alongside the easy or moderate route. This trail characteristic is identified in this section.

The technical ratings used in the trail descriptions are: easy, easy/moderate, moderate, moderate/technical and technical.

ACCESS

This section lists the recommended access route for the trail being described, together with any alternates that might also be suitable.

TRAIL DESCRIPTION

Each trail segment is described in this section at greater length than in the summary. The description covers access details, trail conditions, scenic and other highlights, worthwhile spur trails where these exist, and other points of interest. In no case are such descriptions complete. Many details and highlights are left for bikers to discover for themselves, but enough are given to help those with limited time to select suitable trails, and to provide a few points to watch for along the way. With loop trails, the descriptions begin at the loop-end that is recommended as a starting point. Bikers should consider all mileages noted in this section as approximate, since cyclometer accuracies vary.

OPTIONS

Options suggest additional or alternate routes or trail segments that may be of interest to bikers with varying equipment, time, interests and stamina.

NOTES

Miscellaneous useful information related to each trail is listed in this final section of the trail description format.

STRIP MAP

A topographic strip map is provided with each trail described, showing the trail and the recommended access point. For more information about how the trail relates to other trails and access roads, bikers should refer to the area maps listed at the beginning of the trail description under MAPS.

REPRESENTATIVE PHOTOGRAPHS

With each trail description, photographs show representative or special views along the trail. Other photographs throughout the book show additional regional views and highlights.

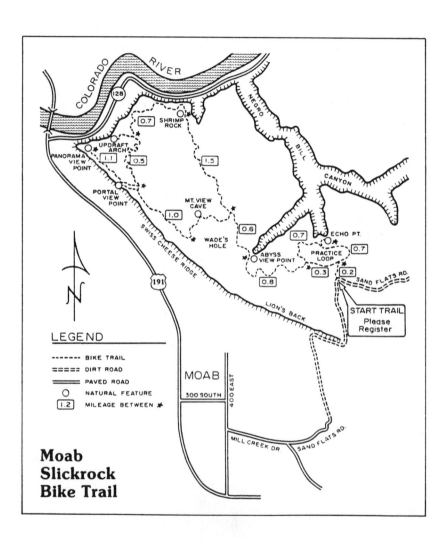

COLORADO RIVER

128

0.7 SHRIMP ROCK

NEGRO

UPDRAFT ARCH

PANORAMA VIEW POINT

1.1 0.5

1.5

BILL

CANYON

PORTAL VIEW POINT

1.0

MT. VIEW CAVE

SWISS CHEESE RIDGE

191

WADE'S HOLE

0.6

0.7 ECHO PT.

PRACTICE LOOP 0.7

ABYSS VIEW POINT

0.3 0.2

0.8

SAND FLATS RD.

LION'S BACK

START TRAIL
Please Register

N

LEGEND

- - - - - BIKE TRAIL
= = = = = DIRT ROAD
───────── PAVED ROAD
○ NATURAL FEATURE
1.2 MILEAGE BETWEEN ✳

MOAB

300 SOUTH

400 EAST

MILL CREEK DR. SAND FLATS RD.

Moab Slickrock Bike Trail

MOAB SLICKROCK BIKE TRAIL

The Moab Slickrock Bike Trail lies above Moab, Utah, on an elevated, six-square-mile mesa of rolling, buff-colored Navajo sandstone. The trail has been likened to a frozen ocean, a petrified rollercoaster, but regardless of metaphor, it does possess a unique combination of qualities which place the trail in a class unto itself.

When first designed for motorcyclists in 1969, no one then could have envisioned its future as the most famous mountain-bike trail in the world. It is basically a strenuous, technically exacting 10-mile loop, with several optional spurs to viewpoints and points of interest. The 2.3-mile, slightly less demanding practice loop is used as a trail sampler, or warm-up.

The average time required to bike the Slickrock Trail is 4 hours, but 5 to 6 hours should be allowed for first encounters. There is negligible net elevation change, but the trail is distinguished by many 5- to 50-foot ascents and descents, defined by potholes, sand traps, and out-of-bounds gardens of vegetated cryptogamic soil.

The trail is 2-1/2 miles from Moab on the Sand Flats Road. There is parking at the trailhead, plus informational signs and a BLM trail register. A BLM trail brochure is available at several locations in Moab and at BLM offices. The various trail loops are marked with broken white lines on the relatively smooth sandstone trail surfaces. The liberal use of paint in an otherwise pristine setting is at first a bit of a shock, but this is probably preferable to alternative signing methods.

There are also painted directional and caution signs. White/yellow and wholly yellow trail markers signify "danger - proceed with caution." The BLM is not an alarmist organization and these should be taken seriously. The entire area is defined by the precipitous Negro Bill and Colorado River canyons, and Moab Valley. There are also myriad opportunities for nasty wipe-outs on this extensive "ocean" of rolling sandstone.

There are no special equipment requirements for the trail. Slightly deflated ordinary tires provide excellent traction on this sandstone, rain or shine. ("Slickrock" is a slightly misleading term. The word was allegedly coined by early-day teamsters, whose shod horses had trouble negotiating sandstone inclines.) A helmet and gloves are essential. Elbow and knee-pads are only seen occasionally and are a matter of preference.

There is extensive dispersed camping available near this trail and along several miles of the Sand Flats Road beyond the trailhead to the lower trailhead of the Porcupine Rim Trail. The area receives heavy recreational use, so care should be taken not to further mar this high desert paradise, neither with tracks nor refuse. The trail is designated for ATVs and motorcycles, and these are occasionally encountered. A segment of the trail is part of a locally popular jeep trail, and vehicles are sometimes met grinding up the fins in the western section.

There are a few assorted caveats which need to be mentioned: bikers need to be willing to push a bike on much of this trail -- up many ascents and through the occasional sand traps. This is considered an integral part of "riding" the trail and should be done shamelessly.

On many of the descents, it is necessary to have body weight as far back as possible over the rear wheel, and a steady hand with the brakes.

Rain or moisture does not seriously affect traction, but the painted trail markers become slippery when wet, so should be avoided. In winter, snow or hoarfrost sometimes stays on the north-facing inclines through the day. This is not a consistent occurrence, but the trail is treacherous when it occurs.

In the high desert, off-trail impacts are far more ecologically destructive than in other environments. The environs may seem to be a barren wasteland, but actually they are teeming with graceful and tenacious life forms which deserve respect. The rule is: "no tracks anywhere off-trail."

That rather basic information aside, what are the characteristics of this highly-touted area which set it so apart? A few are: the trail is largely two equally strenuous but different trails; it can be biked in either direction, with each representing its own set of challenges. Also, the sandstone trail and foundation strata are not affected by measurable erosion. This, coupled with relatively benign winters, results in an irreplaceably constant trail, season after season and year after year, even including the slow-growing, evergreen trailside vegetation. These factors allow the Slickrock Trail to be more a "course" than a trail -- a gymnasium where skills are learned and honed, and their acquisition noted in the relative time and ease with which the course is circled.

Ironically, the surrounding surreal scenery becomes temporarily secondary to the patch of trail surface 30 feet ahead of one's bicycle. Were the Slickrock Trail in the middle of a midwestern wheat field, it would still be a mountain bike mecca. Its actual setting makes it a national treasure.

Trailhead, Moab Slickrock Bike Trail

Mill Creek, Flat Pass/Mill Creek trail

TWENTY-THREE GOOD TRAILS

Choosing twenty-three trails from among all the trails in this region was not easy, because all the named and mapped trails in canyon country are worth traveling. That is why they acquired names and were placed on the commercial maps of the region.

However, for bikers who have only time for sampling one or a few trails, some guidance in selecting the ones to take should be helpful. Virtually every mountain biker will first want to try Moab's Slickrock Bike Trail. This an excellent place to get accustomed to some of the different kinds of trail surfaces that occur in this desert sandstone region.

The next trail that is handy to try is the Sand Flats trail, the graded dirt road that leads to the Slickrock Bike Trail. This can easily be biked for many miles, as it climbs the immense, tilted mesaland defined by Moab Valley, Castle Valley, the La Sal Mountains and the Colorado River gorge.

Beyond the spring-filled water tank that stands on a narrow ridge between upper Negro Bill and Rill canyons, this easy road becomes much steeper and rougher, and it is still many miles before it reaches the paved La Sal Mountain Loop Road. This should be considered before going beyond the spring.

The trails described in detail in this chapter of the book are thus just highlights, trails to check out first before going on to the many others also worth traveling. Most of the other named trails in the region covered by this book are listed in charts in the OTHER TRAILS chapter. The charts provide basic information for each trail listed, together with the names of the ORV books and maps that describe them in more detail.

Bikers who have tried the trails described in this book will no longer need this guidebook. They will by then have been hooked on canyon country, know where else they want to bike, and will be sharing their enthusiasm for this land with others.

For convenience in planning, the trails in this chapter are listed by area. Some of the trails are combinations of access roads and named ORV trails that are particularly suited to mountain biking as loops or continuous routes. In order to avoid name confusion, the trail names used in this book are those standardized on this region's published ORV trail books and maps, except where previously unnamed routes are described. Then, names were assigned, based on nearby geographic features that bear names on U.S. Geological Survey topographic maps.

With each of the six distinct geographic areas, the access roads that serve them are listed, and the general topography is described, before the selected trails are outlined, as an introduction to the land through which the trails travel, and as an aid to planning logistics.

ENJOY!

ARCHES AREA

AREA TERRAIN

This area is defined by Interstate 70 on the north, U.S.191 on the west and Utah 128 on the south and east, and includes all of Arches National Park.

In general, the Arches Area is high, arid to semi-arid desert, broken by immense sandstone uplifts and ridges, slashed by broad valleys and shallow washes and cut deeply by several major canyon systems. The wide variety of geologic formations found in the area provide color, and diversity of shape in land forms, with corresponding variations in trail surfaces.

Within the Arches Area there are two distinct kinds of terrain, each with its own type of scenic beauty and special highlights.

The northern half of the area is relatively flat, open country dominated by colorless seabottom shale interspersed with alluvial sand and gravel, dune sand and outcroppings of sandstone. This area will be of interest to collectors seeking sealife fossils and other minerals, and contains a series of trail segments and spurs that provide access to a number of old mines, springs and other natural features.

The southern half of the Arches Area contains most of this area's scenic highlights. Its rugged highlands are studded with still higher outcroppings of colorful sandstone and are slashed deeply in many places by complex canyon systems that eventually drain into the Colorado River gorge. Gigantic red and white sandstone uplifts border broad Salt Valley, and immense sandstone fins, domes, spires, buttes and arches create unmatched panoramas within the area now protected in Arches National Park.

ACCESS ROADS

Access to the Arches Area is from its perimeter highways, I-70, U.S.191 and Utah 128, and by way of the one paved road into Arches National Park, plus a few graded dirt roads.

Arches Road. This paved road leaves U.S.191 about 2-1/2 miles north of the Colorado River bridge, enters Arches National Park, climbs steeply onto higher terrain then continues northward within the park, to end about 17 miles from U.S.191. This is the primary access route into the park, and also provides access to several off-road vehicle trail segments.

Thompson Road. This graded dirt road heads south from Thompson, goes beneath I-70, then angles southwestward to connect with U.S. 191 about 5 miles south of Crescent Junction. The terrain this road travels is relatively colorless, featureless desert, but it provides access to two major trail segments.

Yellowcat Road. This graded dirt road goes southeast from an I-70 interchange about 11 miles east of Crescent Junction, and connects with a major trail segment, the Yellowcat trail. The road crosses relatively featureless desert, but is useful for access to the Arches Area from the north.

Pinto Wash Road. This graded dirt road goes south from a gravel frontage road, about 2 miles west of the Cisco interchange on I-70. From there, the road crosses open desert cut by several drywashes, to connect with the Yellowcat trail about 5 miles east of the junction of Yellowcat Road with Yellowcat trail.

INTRODUCTION

The best mountain-bike trails in the Arches area are not in Arches National Park. Many people want to bike there but, unfortunately, there are only two good stretches of biking trail in the park. Bikers who use the park's paved roads will be distracted and endangered by highway vehicles. There are no special biking trails or routes in the park.

The unpaved roads in Arches are either very sandy, are uninteresting from a technical viewpoint, or both, and they are no more scenic than the paved road.

One trail segment in the park worth biking is the stretch of Willow Spring trail within the park, and even this is only modestly scenic. The other segment is the Eye-of-the-Whale Trail, to and a little beyond the hiking trail to that curious arch. Dune and wash sand make the rest of the trail unbikable.

Backcountry permits are required for overnight camping in Arches National Park, except in the campground, and bikes are not allowed on foot trails or off the park roads and ORV trails.

Only one trail has been described in the general Arches area. While several of the others are highly scenic, they are remote and too long for casual biking, and most have long sandy stretches. Bikers who wish to explore these trails should plan to do so from a base camp somewhere in the Yellowcat area to the east of Arches National Park.

TRAIL NAME: Klondike Bluffs

TRAIL SUMMARY: This trail gently ascends the western incline of the Salt Valley Anticline, beginning in painted desert-type scenery. It then crosses a broad expanse of white sandstone and enters an elevated valley set with pinyon and juniper trees. It ends at a high viewpoint in Arches National Park, overlooking the Klondike Bluffs and other scenic areas of the park.

TRAIL TYPE: spur.   LAND OWNERSHIP: BLM & NPS

MAP: *Canyon Country* OFF-ROAD VEHICLE TRAIL MAP, <u>Arches & La Sals Areas</u>

MILEAGES: 16 miles round trip, about 10 miles if the ride is begun at the major fork 2-3/4 miles in from U.S.191.

TIME REQUIRED: 4 hours, longer if time is spent exploring the Klondike Bluffs area on foot, or if spur trails are explored.

BEST SEASON: This is an all-season trail, except during periods of wet weather, when the first 3-1/2 miles of clay road become treacherous to all vehicles, especially in late winter and early spring, or following summer rain.

DIFFICULTY: easy/moderate, with packed sediments, packed drift sand, broad avenues of slickrock, and a little wash sand. The trail gradually gains 700 feet over its length.

TECHNICAL RATING: easy, with optional moderate slickrock expanses. Good trail for varying levels of experience.

ACCESS: The trailhead is 20 minutes from Moab by vehicle. Drive north on U.S.191 to 5.4 miles beyond the turnoff to Dead Horse Point and Canyonlands National Park (U313). The trail is described below from where it leaves U.S.191, but bikers can reduce the time and mileage by driving the first 2-3/4 miles to the first major trail junction.

TRAIL DESCRIPTION:

From the highway, the trail goes immediately through a fenceline, then winds eastward for two miles through barren, colorless terrain. The white-capped fins and towers of Klondike Bluffs come into view as the trail drops into Little Valley.

The trail forks at about 2-3/4 miles. If driving, this is the place to park. The left fork is the trail. It travels northward, closely paralleling colorful hills on the left. After the trail crosses the wash sand of Little Valley, it forks. Here, the trail goes right, and in less than 1/4 mile comes to another spur to the left. There, the trail continues straight ahead, to enter a narrow, rocky canyon, where a variety of vegetation thrives on the moisture in the drainage.

The trail emerges from this canyon onto a broad, rising slope of white slickrock -- the Moab member of the Entrada formation. This point is about 4-1/2 miles from the trail start at U.S.191. The trail ascends the slickrock slope, closely following a wall of reddish sediments on the left, as it snakes upward through a corridor of large boulders.

Farther along, the trail passes a large balanced rock on the left, above the red embankment. About 150 yards beyond this landmark, there are a number of dinosaur tracks beside the trail. These may be protected from wheels by a line of branches. Just beyond this point, the sediment interface drops downward to the left, while the trail continues ahead across the slickrock.

At this point, it becomes necessary to use the navigation tactics noted earlier in this book. Watch for wheel tracks in small patches of soil. These will guide you across the next 1/2 mile or so of slickrock, until the trail again becomes obvious and levels out. Shortly, a spur trail comes in from the left. In less than 1/4 mile, another spur ascends the rocky valley rim, but the main trail goes right.

In about another 1/4 mile, another fork appears. Go left here. In another 1/2 mile, continue straight ahead where a spur goes right to the visible remains of an old copper-mining operation. The trail then winds up a very rough, rubbly slope, comes to an Arches National Park boundary marker, then continues up this eroded mining trail to where it tops out and ends in another 1/4 mile. At this point, you are in the park.

On this high plateau, the view south is across painted desert toward the Monitor and Merrimac buttes in Courthouse Pasture. Toward the northwest, the tilted, jagged teeth of the San Rafael Reef are visible in the distance on clear days.

To the east is Salt Valley. Across the valley are the red sandstone fins and domes of Eagle Park, the Fiery Furnace and the Devils Garden, with the highlands of Dome Plateau beyond. Toward the southeast are the Klondike Bluffs. Beyond these spectacular fins are the petrified dunes and Courthouse Towers of Arches, and beyond those are the low domes of the Slickrock Bike Trail and the Moab Rim, on the far side of the Colorado River.

The ride back is an easy 1-1/2 hours, even allowing for some time spent playing in the slickrock areas near the trail.

NOTES:

1. It is possible to explore the Klondike Bluffs area on foot from the overlook. Follow the white caprock down toward the west, and then around into the red slickrock.

2. The old copper mine site is interesting. A cinder block there hides a very deep drill-hole that penetrates an underground cavern that contains water.

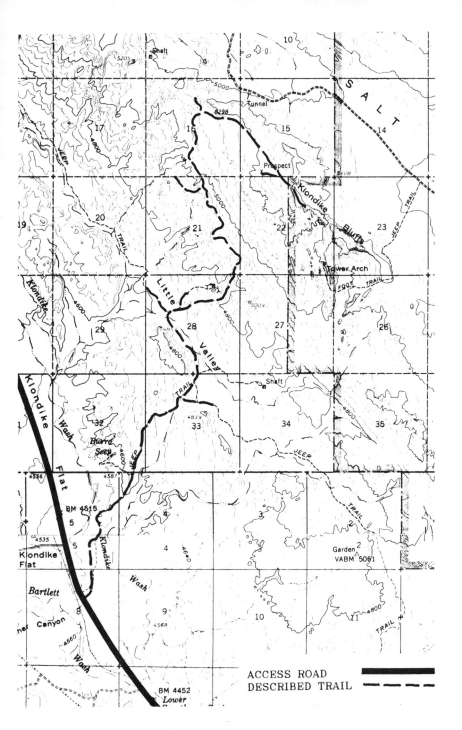

ACCESS ROAD
DESCRIBED TRAIL

KLONDIKE BLUFFS TRAIL MAP

Klondike Bluffs trail

Klondike Bluffs viewpoint

CANYON RIMS AREA

AREA TERRAIN

This area is defined by U.S.191 on the east, the Colorado River on the west and Utah 211 and lower Indian Creek Canyon on the south. It includes all of the Bureau of Land Management's Canyon Rims Recreation Area.

The Canyon Rims Area contains three types of terrain. One lies between Moab Valley and Cane Creek Canyon. This area is extremely distorted, eroded and spectacular, with deep canyons, great masses of slickrock domes and fins and a few relatively level sandflats. It is known locally as "Behind the Rocks" because it is "behind" the southwestern wall of Moab Valley.

The second distinct type of terrain occupies the eastern and central section of the area, and is essentially high, rolling desert studded with scattered outcroppings of colorful slickrock and cut by a complex of shallow washes and canyons. This desert is terminated on the south, west and northeast by a series of deep canyons and enormous cliffs.

The third type of terrain in this area lies between these cliffs and the rim of the Colorado River gorge. Most of it is strangely eroded dark red sandstone and sediments and red-sand desert, studded with colorful rock outcroppings and cut by a series of deep, labyrinthine canyons that ultimately join the Colorado River gorge.

ACCESS ROADS

Access to the Canyon Rims Area from its perimeter highways, U.S.191 and Utah 211, is by way of one road that is partly paved and partly graveled, and another paved road that has a gravel road spur.

Cane Creek Road. This paved road leaves U.S.191 (Main Street) five blocks south of the center of Moab (Center Street). It provides access to a major subdivision, then parallels the cliffs to the southwest of Moab before entering the Colorado River gorge. There, it travels downriver between the river and cliffs for about 3 miles before entering lower Cane Creek Canyon. The pavement ends just before the road enters the canyon. The road is graveled from there on to where it ends, about 7 miles up Cane Creek Canyon. Cane Creek Road is considered to end where it reaches a ford of Cane Creek, because this crossing is often not passable to 2-wheel-drive vehicles. As the road continues beyond the Cane Creek ford, it is called the Hurrah Pass trail in this book. This road makes a good mountain-bike route.

Needles Overlook Road. This paved road leaves U.S.191 about 33 miles south of Moab, and about 12 miles south of La Sal Junction. The road penetrates the Canyon Rims Recreation Area, passes Wind Whistle Campground, then ends at the Needles Overlook, an outstanding plateau rim viewpoint.

Anticline Overlook Road. This good graveled road spurs north from the Needles Overlook Road about 16 miles from U.S.191. It travels the high mesa-top of Hatch Point. About 9 miles from this junction, a 1-mile spur road goes east to Hatch Point Campground. A short spur road to the west beyond the campground junction goes to a colorful viewpoint above the Colorado River gorge. The main road ends at Anticline Overlook, which offers a spectacular view down into the lower canyon country that surrounds this lofty vantage point. This road makes an easy but very scenic mountain-bike route.

Anticline Overlook

TRAIL NAME: Amasa Back.

TRAIL SUMMARY: This trail leaves Cane Creek road, crosses Cane Creek Canyon and immediately ascends a series of moderately technical sandstone ledges onto an immense sandstone ridge isolated by the Colorado River gorge and Cane Creek Canyon. There are many outstanding views along this trail.

TRAIL TYPE: spur.   LAND OWNERSHIP: BLM

MAP: *Canyon Country* OFF-ROAD VEHICLE TRAIL MAP, Canyon Rims & Needles Areas.

MILEAGES: 9 miles round trip, plus 2 miles for an optional spur.

TIME REQUIRED: 3 hours.

BEST SEASON: all-season trail.

DIFFICULTY: moderate/strenuous. The trail gains 800 feet in the first 2-1/2 miles. The trail surface is primarily packed sediments and slickrock ledges, and some packed drift sand toward the end of the trail.

TECHNICAL RATING: moderate.

ACCESS: From Moab, drive or bike on Cane Creek road to the pavement end, about 4-1/2 miles from U.S.191 (Main St.) in Moab. Continue on the graveled road 1.1 miles to where this trail drops steeply into Cane Creek Canyon.

Eric Bajon photo

39

TRAIL DESCRIPTION:

The trail immediately descends a series of rocky ledges and slopes to Cane Creek, a perennially flowing stream. The trail crosses the creek and ascends the canyon wall on rocky ledges and terraces for the first mile or so.

Funnel Arch is visible at points along the first 2 miles of this trail. The arch is high on a terrace above Cane Creek road, on the opposite side of the canyon.

About 2 miles beyond the creek, the trail forks on a bare patch of slickrock. The main trail goes right to skirt the bases of three monoliths. The left fork is an interesting spur that ends in a lovely, box-end canyon in about 1 mile.

The main trail continues to ascend more gently. Near its summit, it skirts the lofty rim of Jackson Hole, a "rincon," or abandoned meander of the Colorado River. Shortly after the trail passes the most ledgy, exposed section, it comes to a right spur that goes to a spectacular view across the Colorado River gorge.

About 3/4 mile beyond this spur, the trail crosses a gas pipeline, which descends the western slope of Amasa Back to the potash plant downriver. The main trail continues on the Amasa Back ridge for about 1 mile, to where free biking or hiking becomes necessary to further explore the Amasa Back peninsula.

Amasa Back trail, around the rim of Jackson Hole

40

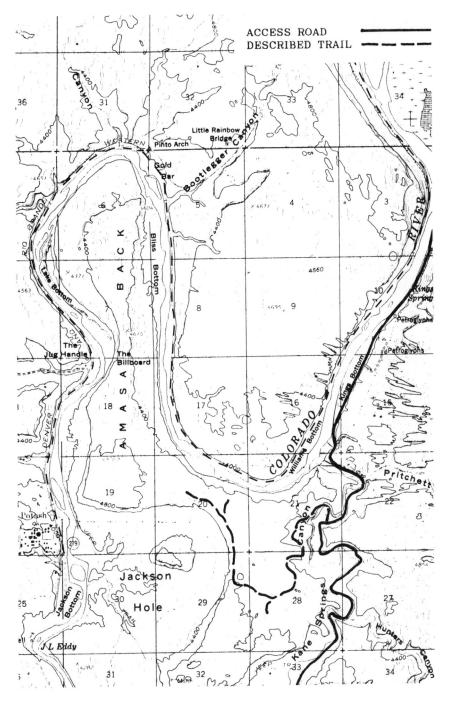

AMASA BACK TRAIL MAP

41

Amasa Back trail view   Tom Kuehne photo

Funnel Arch

TRAIL NAME: Cane Creek Canyon Rim/Pritchett Canyon. Jan '94

TRAIL SUMMARY: This favorite trail crosses packed drift sand for the first 4 miles in the southeastern part of Behind-the-Rocks, then ascends to and closely parallels the high eastern rim of spectacular Cane Creek Canyon for several miles. The trail then descends into upper Hunter Canyon, climbs out of that drainage system, then descends wild and beautiful Pritchett Canyon to Cane Creek Road, 4-1/2 miles downriver of Moab.

TRAIL TYPE: connecting.   Land Ownership: BLM

MAP: *Canyon Country* OFF-ROAD VEHICLE TRAIL MAP, Canyon Rims & Needles Areas.

MILEAGE: about 22 miles, more if various spurs are explored.

TIME REQUIRED: 5-7 hours.

BEST SEASON: all-season trail. During very dry weather, add about 1 hour to the time suggested, due to some wash sand.

DIFFICULTY: moderate. The trail crosses a variety of terrain, including packed drift sand, packed rocky sediments, packed wash sand and some deep wash sand. The trail loses 1500 feet.

TECHNICAL RATING: moderate, with minimal technical stretches.

ACCESS: 15 minutes from Moab by vehicle. The trail spurs to the west from U.S.191 near the top of the Blue Hill summit, 5.1 miles south of the La Sal Mountain Loop Road turnoff, and about 12 miles south of Moab. The trail is described from that point, but except in very wet or very dry conditions, carefully driven 2-wheel-drive vehicles can travel the first few miles of the trail.

Cane Creek Canyon rim viewpoint

43

TRAIL DESCRIPTION:

From U.S.191, the trail crosses a cattle guard, passes a couple of spurs to the right in the first 1/2 mile, then reaches an obvious junction at about 3 miles. The left spur goes west to upper Cane Creek Canyon rim. The main trail goes ahead to another fork, goes left and continues toward a sandstone butte.

At this butte, a spur right goes to Balcony Arch, then around the butte to Picture Frame Arch. Both are worth seeing.

Back on the main trail, just beyond an impressive panorama of Behind-the-Rocks and the La Sals, the trail descends into a sandy washbottom. It then skirts a tributary of upper Cane Creek Canyon for a couple of miles, while ascending toward the eastern rim of that canyon. The trail then parallels Cane Creek Canyon rim and passes several spurs to rim viewpoints.

The trail next swings to the right and begins a steep descent into upper Hunter Canyon, passing a spur to the right. About 3/4 mile past this spur is a fork to the right, where the main trail is temporarily inconspicuous because it crosses a short stretch of bare slickrock. Cairns may mark the trail here.

About 14-1/4 miles from the trailhead, the trail drops into the wash of upper Hunter Canyon. A short distance down the wash, it plunges down a pour-off through a small natural bridge.

Beyond the wash, the main trail soon reaches the spur to the Pritchett Arch hiking trailhead, about where the upper part of Pritchett Arch is visible. The marked foot trail to the arch climbs a steep slope to the rim, then bears right along the rim, passing Cummings Arch enroute to Pritchett Arch and, across a sandy valley, Wigwam Arch. For an excellent view down Pritchett Canyon, hike beyond Pritchett Arch.

Beyond the Pritchett Arch spur, the main trail passes a rock spire, then climbs out of the Hunter Canyon drainage to the summit of infamous "Yellow Hill," so named for coloring mineral deposits. This summit is 16.2 miles from the trail's head, and 4-1/2 miles from its end. Beyond this summit, the trail descends Yellow Hill into Pritchett Canyon. At the base of the grade, a spur left goes to a hiking trail to Halls Bridge, but the main trail continues downcanyon between Ostrich Rock and Window Arch.

On down the canyon, a right spur goes up a sidecanyon, to Troll Bridge and an arch high in a sandstone fin at the end of the spur, but the main trail continues downcanyon, eventually to end at Cane Creek Road, about 4-1/2 miles from Moab.

NOTES:

1. Entering Pritchett Canyon from its lower end, biking up the canyon, hiking to Pritchett Arch, then returning by the same route makes an excellent and challenging one-day trip.

2. Taking this trail as described, then returning to its beginning via the paved roads, makes a loop trip of about 38 miles, with 16-1/2 miles on pavement.

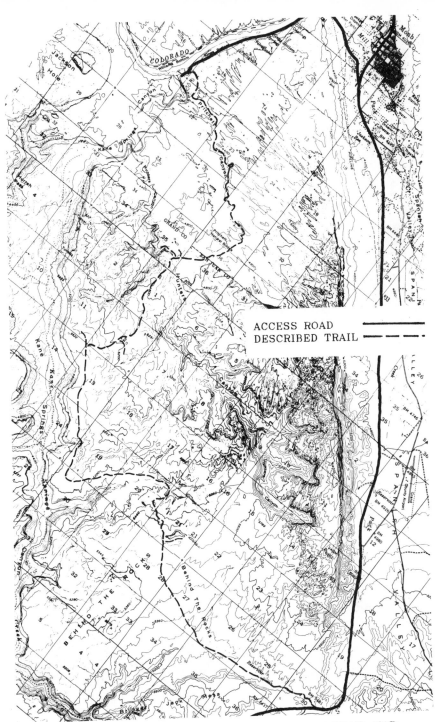

ACCESS ROAD
DESCRIBED TRAIL

CANE CREEK CANYON RIM/PRITCHETT CANYON TRAIL MAP

Summit of Yellow Hill   Tom Kuehne photo

Pritchett Arch

TRAIL NAME: Hurrah Pass/Chicken Corners.

TRAIL SUMMARY: This trail ascends the colorful sloping strata of an anticline to Hurrah Pass, then descends to travel the rim of the Colorado River gorge, ending at a spectacular rim viewpoint south of Dead Horse Point, on the opposite side of the river.

TRAIL TYPE: spur.   LAND OWNERSHIP: BLM

MAP: *Canyon Country* OFF-ROAD VEHICLE TRAIL MAP, Canyon Rims & Needles Areas

MILEAGE: 30 miles round trip.

BEST SEASON: all-season trail, but accumulates snow during the winter months. Some soft sand during very dry seasons.

TIME REQUIRED: 7 hours.

DIFFICULTY: mainly easy, with packed sediments and drift sand. Some bikers may have to walk parts of the grades to the summit of Hurrah Pass, which is 600 feet above the trailhead.

TECHNICAL RATING: easy.

ACCESS: 25 minutes from Moab by vehicle. Drive 4-1/2 miles from Moab on Cane Creek Road, to the end of the pavement, then another 6-1/4 miles to the Cane Creek ford. See OPTION.

Petroglyphs, Cane Creek Road

47

TRAIL DESCRIPTION:

The trail begins at the Cane Creek ford. In less than 1/2 mile, the Cane Creek Canyon trail spurs left, while this trail swings to the right and ascends the western slopes of Cane Creek Canyon, offering outstanding views down into that colorful gorge. The trail winds through huge buttes and towers of Cutler and Moenkopi sandstones, capped with greenish-gray Chinle sediments.

The trail continues through this eroded, colorful maze to the summit of Hurrah Pass, and its outstanding panorama. Cane Creek Canyon dominates toward the east, with the La Sals visible above its lofty rim. To the north are the slickrock domes and fins of the Moab Rim. To the west and southwest are the Island-in-the-Sky, Dead Horse Point and Grand View Point. Across the Colorado River gorge are the Great Pyramid, the solar evaporation ponds, and the great upswelling of Cane Creek Anticline. The display pavilion of Anticline Overlook is visible high above.

The trail descends from the summit, following the cliffline, then goes down a rough alluvial slope toward the distant river bluff. Some 2-1/2 miles from the pass summit, the Jackson Hole trail spurs right down a shallow gulch through a fenceline, while the main trail continues ahead in the main wash. Within a short distance, the trail leaves this wash by ascending a steep, bare slickrock slope, then continuing toward the river bluff.

For a couple of miles the trail parallels the river, past short spurs that go down washes or to rim overlooks. About 2-1/4 miles from the Jackson Hole spur, there are two spurs to the left. These lead to a large sandstone mass which is riddled with natural caves. Be on the alert for rattlesnakes in these caves during warmer months.

The main trail continues parallel to the river, rounding the heads of several tributary canyons that are rimmed with a gray limestone that contains sea-life fossils, skirting along the base of a convoluted red sandstone bluff until eventually it is forced back to the rivergorge rim by the bluff. There, a narrow stretch of rim-edge trail is called "Chicken Corners." The trail continues beyond this breathtaking stretch for another 1-1/2 miles before ending at a spectacular river gorge overlook opposite Dead Horse Point, and about 450 feet above the river.

OPTION: Strong bikers can easily travel the entire 30-mile trail from the creek ford. Since this ford and the trail to the Hurrah Pass summit are often passable to carefully driven 2-wheel-drive vehicles, one option is to drive to the summit. From there, the round trip will be about 22 miles, and take 5 hours.

NOTES:

1. The short stretch of trail called "Chicken Corners" was given its name by a Moab tour guide because many of his passengers were "chicken" and preferred to walk the more dangerous few yards. This stretch of trail was once far more hazardous than it is now.

2. On the return trip, it is easy to spot a curious natural bridge about 15 feet from the trail and slightly lower. It is flat on top and formed in the hard, gray limestone that rims the rivergorge and its tributaries in this area.

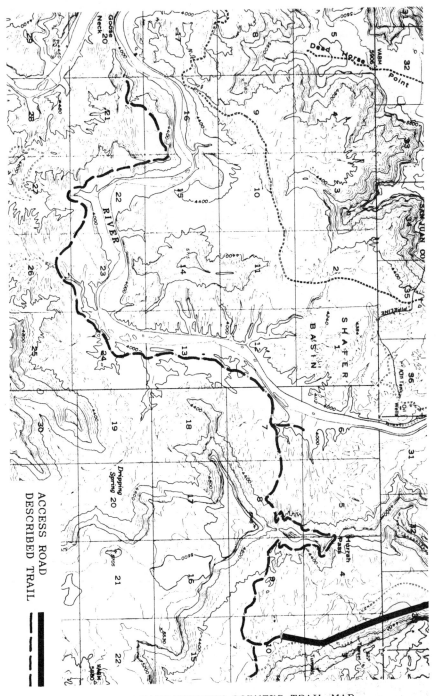

ACCESS ROAD
DESCRIBED TRAIL

HURRAH PASS/CHICKEN CORNERS TRAIL MAP

Cane Creek Canyon from Hurrah Pass summit

Colorado River gorge, from Chicken Corners trail

TRAIL NAME: Moab Rim.

TRAIL SUMMARY: This short but challenging trail climbs into the sandstone fantasyland called "Behind-the-Rocks," part of which may be designated as a wilderness area. It offers views of archeological sites, the Colorado River gorge, Moab Valley, and the highlands of Arches National Park. In either direction, the trail is a workout. The first mile climbs 800 feet, and was the route of the 1986 Fat Tire Festival Hill Climb event. This trail, and the hiking trail that continues beyond its end, are both designated BLM hiking routes.

TRAIL TYPE: spur.   OWNERSHIP: BLM

MAP: *Canyon Country* OFF-ROAD VEHICLE TRAIL MAP, Canyon Rims & Needles Areas.

MILEAGE: 9 miles round trip, more if the spurs are taken.

TIME REQUIRED: 3-1/2 hours. Allow more for exploration.

BEST SEASON: all-season trail, except when snow is on it.

DIFFICULTY: Strenuous. The trail gains 900 feet of elevation on ledgy slickrock, sand, and rubble, with many low climbs and descents even after the rim is gained.

TECHNICAL RATING: technical.

ACCESS: 5 minutes from Moab by vehicle, or 10 minutes by bike. The trailhead is 2.6 miles from Main Street (U.S.191) on Cane Creek Road, and is 0.2 mile beyond the first cattle guard. A BLM sign marks the trailhead.

View down the first mile, Moab Rim trail

TRAIL DESCRIPTION:

There is a BLM register near the trail head. Spray-painted arrows mark the route to the rim, where the trail then turns right to parallel the rim. In the inaugural Fat Tire Festival of 1986, the winning time to this point was 13:7.

In 1/2 mile, the trail turns away from the rim and in another 1/4 mile reaches a fork, where Buttress Arch is visible to the left. The trail goes right, and in 1/3 mile crosses a shallow slickrock arroyo with small potholes visible downstream. This wash plunges into Moonflower Canyon, a sidecanyon of the Colorado, and is worth hiking. A hike along the right rim of this wash leads to beautiful views of the Colorado River gorge and the first steep stretch of this trail.

Beyond the arroyo, the trail continues through sand and rock, then ascends a huge slickrock dome, the top of which is the halfway point of this trail. The 360-degree panorama from here includes the La Sal Mountains, the fins of Behind-the-Rocks, the rim of Cane Creek Canyon with Hurrah Pass beyond, Amasa Back, Airport Tower, Long Canyon, the Bull Canyon system, Gold Bar rim, the highlands in Arches, and the formation called "The Armchair."

The trail then pitches steeply down the sandstone dome in the general direction of The Armchair and passes several more spurs to various features. A little more than a mile beyond the dome, the trail comes to a sandy washbottom where a left spur climbs toward The Armchair and a Moab Rim viewpoint. The main trail continues straight up the grade and ends 1 mile later at the upper end of the BLM's Hidden Valley Hiking Trail.

Near the trail's end, there are many petroglyphs along the base of the high sandstone ridge above the trail. The easiest way to see them is to hike the BLM trail 1/3 mile, to where it overlooks upper Hidden Valley, then turn left and climb to the ridge. Sadly, many of the petroglyphs have been vandalized.

NOTES:

1. At the trailhead, Little Arch, high on the opposite rim of the river, is accessible via the Poison Spider Mesa trail.

2. On the return trip, it is easy to take a wrong turn on a patch of slickrock, about 1-1/4 miles from trail's end, and go down a steep, sandy slope. Even though this route does rejoin the main trail, avoid it by keeping left here.

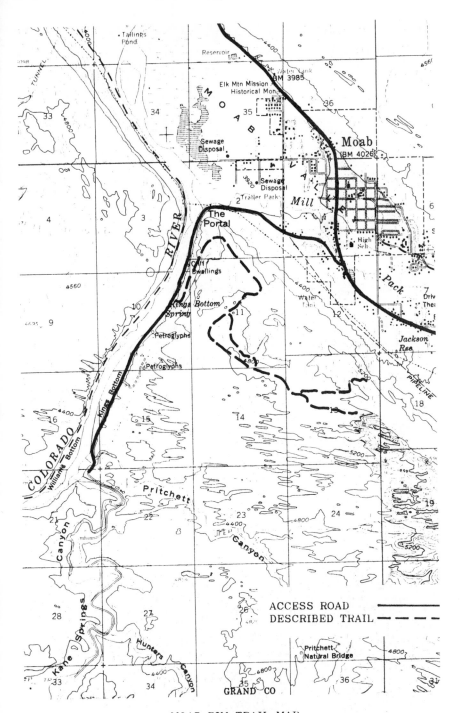

ACCESS ROAD ━━━━━━
DESCRIBED TRAIL ━ ━ ━

MOAB RIM TRAIL MAP

53

Prehistoric rock art, near Moab Rim trail

The Bureau of Land Management's Canyon Rims Recreation Area offers two campgrounds -- Wind Whistle and Hatch Point -- two plateau-rim developments -- Needles Overlook and Anticline Overlook -- and paved and graveled roads that provide access to these locations. Graded dirt roads and ORV trails provide access to the spectacular canyons that slash this elevated plateauland.

The following trails were selected to give bikers a sample of the scenic beauty this recreation area offers that cannot be visited by highway vehicle.

The first trail gives a glimpse of the immense Harts Draw canyon system. An American exploring party descended a tributary of this canyon in 1859, and became the first to view and describe the area now in Canyonlands National Park. The upper end of an historic stock route into the canyon leaves this trail just before it climbs onto the elevated plateau where it ends.

The second trail offers a sample of another type of terrain that is unique to this area, plus views into Hatch Wash, another major canyon system that cuts through the area. Neither trail is particularly demanding, but both sample the wild natural beauty of this recreation area, from the convenient base of Wind Whistle Campground.

Wind Whistle Campground

TRAIL NAME: Wind Whistle I.

TRAIL SUMMARY: This short trail climbs onto a high peninsula between two tributary canyons of spectacular Harts Draw.

TRAIL TYPE: spur.   LAND OWNERSHIP: BLM

MAP: *Canyon Country* OFF-ROAD VEHICLE TRAIL MAP, Canyon Rims & Needles Areas. The trail described is not shown on this map, but its access roads are.

MILEAGE: 4-1/2 miles round trip.

TIME REQUIRED: 1 hour.

BEST SEASON: three-season trail, when dry.

DIFFICULTY: easy/moderate. The trail gains 250 feet.

TECHNICAL RATING: easy/moderate.

ACCESS: About 32 miles south of Moab on U.S.191, about 45 minutes from Moab by vehicle, turn onto the paved road into the Canyon Rims Recreation Area. Wind Whistle Campground is 5-1/2 miles from the highway on this road. The trail leaves the pavement 0.6 miles beyond Wind Whistle Campground.

TRAIL DESCRIPTION:

The trail winds through rolling sand hills for 1/2 mile to a fork. The left fork ends at the base of Wind Whistle Rock. The main trail goes right, and continues through packed drift sand and across occasional exposures of sandstone, providing distant views of a deep tributary canyon.

It then ascends onto a flat-topped plateau, descends to travel a narrow peninsula, then climbs onto another plateau, where it ends at an overlook into Harts Draw and several of its tributaries. A walk around this plateau rim yields stunning views into deep and narrow gorges almost 1,000 feet below.

NOTES:

1. There may be a series of cairns leading down to the left about 1/3 mile before trail's end. These indicate the old cattle trail that is used by hikers to get into Harts Draw.

2. Wind Whistle Campground is a BLM-maintained campground with water available from about May through October. A fee is charged except when the water is off. There are about 20 sites, 14 of them accessible to vehicles.

TRAIL NAME: Wind Whistle II.

TRAIL SUMMARY: This trail penetrates a part of the Canyon Rims Recreation Area that is exceptionally scenic. It travels across broad, grassy meadows that are set with massive domes and plateaus of Navajo sandstone and bordered by deep, spectacular canyons, with excellent hiking many places.

TRAIL TYPE: spur.   LAND OWNERSHIP: BLM

MAPS: *Canyon Country* OFF-ROAD VEHICLE TRAIL MAP, Canyon Rims & Needles Areas, and U.S.G.S. 1:100,000 scale metric map, "La Sal."

MILEAGES: about 31 miles round-trip from Wind Whistle Campground, including one short spur, or about 14 miles round trip from where the trail leaves the graded dirt road.

TIME REQUIRED: about 6 hours from the campground, 3 from the graded road, plus any time spent hiking.

BEST SEASON: May through November, except following rain.

DIFFICULTY: easy. A total elevation change of about 560 feet.

TECHNICAL RATING: easy.

ACCESS: The trail can be biked from Wind Whistle Campground, or from where the ORV part of the trail branches from the graded dirt road, about 8-1/4 miles from the campground. The latter is recommended because the dirt road stretch is rather monotonous.

TRAIL DESCRIPTION:

From Wind Whistle Campground, bike or drive about 1-1/2 miles westward to Soup Rock, a large sandstone dome on the left, and turn right there on a graded dirt road. In another 1-1/2 miles, turn left at a main road junction. From that junction, go about 5-1/4 miles, to where the road dips down through a shallow wash. Just beyond this wash, if biking, turn right onto a branching trail, then right again in a few yards. If driving, park beside the dirt road near the trail junction and begin biking there.

From the dirt road, the trail travels generally northeast and gradually descends into country that steadily becomes more interesting as it enters a region of gigantic sandstone domes, grassy meadows and deep canyons.

About 2-1/2 miles from the graded dirt road, watch for a spur trail to the right that skirts a lofty sandstone peninsula, on terraces that closely skirt a deep tributary canyon of Hatch Wash. This trail rounds the tip of the high mesa, to end on the brink of another tributary. These canyon rims provide good hiking, and it is possible to hike down into both canyons.

The main trail reaches another junction about 1-1/2 miles beyond the spur trail junction. Go right at this second junction for about 1 mile, to where the rim of a canyon is visible about 30 yards to the east, or right, of the trail. This deep and narrow gorge is Hatch Wash, one of the two major canyons that join a few miles farther downstream to become Cane Creek Canyon. For much of the year, the canyon has a flowing stream, with pools, rapids and small cascades. This area also provides good hiking. The return trip along the same route provides other views of the Navajo Meadows area, and other hiking opportunities.

NOTES:

1. Although this trail is listed as a spur, it is possible to make it a loop by heading westward toward the graded dirt road from the last trail junction, rather than retracing the route already traveled. This is not recommended. While this way out travels an easy stretch of trail, the scenery along this route out is quite monotonous, numerous branching trails confuse navigation, and it is longer than returning by the same route.

2. This trail should be avoided following significant amounts of rain or snow, and some sandy stretches become difficult during extremely hot, dry weather. It is most apt to be ideal in late spring, May and June, when wildflowers abound, and late fall, October and November, when autumn-hued grasses turn the meadows gold. Watch for antelope.

Harts Draw Bridge, visible from Wind Whistle I trail

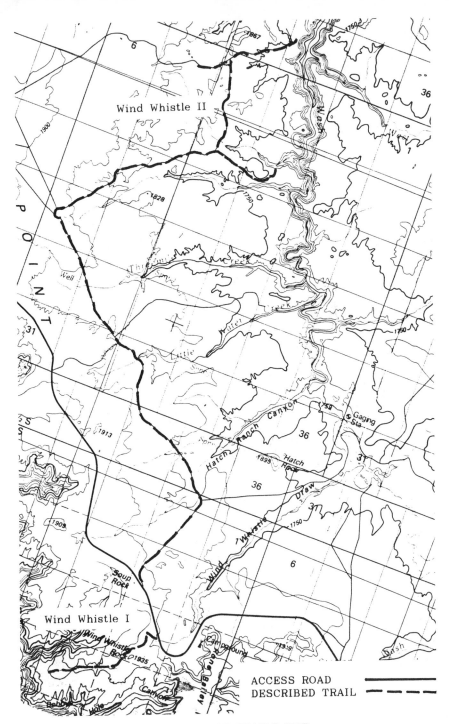

ACCESS ROAD
DESCRIBED TRAIL

WIND WHISTLE TRAILS MAP

59

Determination Towers, Courthouse Pasture

ISLAND AREA

AREA TERRAIN

This area is defined by Interstate 70 on the north, the Green River on the west and U.S.191 and the Colorado River on the east, and includes the Island-in-the-Sky district of Canyonlands National Park.

The Island Area in general is high, arid to semi-arid desert, broken by huge sandstone outcroppings and buttes, and slashed by hundreds of shallow washes, deeper canyons and great, sheer-walled gorges. The wide variety of geologic formations found in the area provide color, diversity of shape in land forms and variations in trail surfaces. The area can be divided into four distinct kinds of terrain, each with its own type of scenic beauty and special highlights.

The northeastern half of the northern third of the area is relatively flat, open country dominated by colorless seabottom shale interspersed with alluvial sand and gravel, dune sand and some outcroppings of older sandstone deposits. This area may be of some interest to collectors seeking sealife fossils, but contains few if any trails of interest to anyone.

The southwestern half of this northern third of the area is more colorful, offers good hunting for mineral collectors and contains a number of trails worth traveling, but does not display the kind of spectacular scenery that dominates the southern two-thirds of the area.

The central portion of the Island Area is broad, open sandflats studded with massive domes, mesas and ridges of red-hued, monolithic sandstone. This high desert also contains several large areas dominated by eroded white sandstone and sand dunes, and is deeply cut by a complex series of huge canyons that radiate in all directions from a low rock promontory called The Knoll. These canyons all eventually join the great gorges of the Green and Colorado rivers. As these gorges converge to their confluence within the heart of Canyonlands National Park, the plateauland narrows to become the long, branching, sheer-walled peninsula called Island-in-the-Sky. Dead Horse Point is another such peninsula.

The fourth type of terrain in the Island Area is found below the high Island-in-the-Sky and adjoining plateau country, on an intermediate level that is still above the Colorado and Green rivers. The unusual white sandstone formation that is the foundation of this immense benchland slopes gradually upward from north to south. It is dominated on one side by the sheer red cliffs and great talus slopes of Island-in-the-Sky and associated highlands. Below the benchland, weirdly eroded, dark red sandstone deposits, cut by hundreds of canyons and gorges, slope away toward the two ancient rivers that define the area.

ACCESS ROADS

Access into the Island Area from its perimeter highways, I-70, U.S.191 and Utah 279, is by way of one paved road, Utah 313, and an interconnecting system of graded dirt roads, most of them not officially named.

Utah 313. This paved road leaves U.S.191 about 8 miles north of the Colorado River bridge, penetrates scenic Sevenmile Canyon, then climbs steeply up onto the high mesa that becomes Island-in-the-Sky farther south. Here, the road crosses open sand flats studded with rounded sandstone outcroppings, with views to the north of massive redrock buttes. The road ends at Dead Horse Point, another slender extension of the same great mesa.

Island Road. This paved road branches from Utah 313 at The Knoll, about 14 miles from U.S.191, and continues south onto the Island-in-the-Sky in Canyonlands National Park, where it branches several times to approach various overlooks and features. After this road enters the park, it offers spectacular distant views of the canyon country to the east, south and west.

Floy Wash Road. This dirt road heads south from I-70 about 13 miles east of the Green River bridge, or about 6 miles west of Crescent Junction. It travels generally southwest through relatively colorless, featureless desert until it reaches the vicinity of White Wash, where it ends at the Green River.

Blue Hills Road. This dirt road heads generally northwest from U.S.191 just south of the airstrip at Canyonlands Field. It travels many miles of colorless, monotonous desert before connecting with the Floy Wash Road 4 miles south of I-70.

Dubinky Well Road. This dirt road travels north and south to connect the Blue Hills Road and Utah 313. It offers scenic beauty along most of its length, and passes Dubinky Well (an old windmill and catch basin) along the way. This road makes an easy but very scenic mountain-bike route.

Duma Point Road. This dirt road leaves the Blue Hills Road about 13 miles from U.S.191, then heads southwest through colorful and interesting geologic formations to become an off-road vehicle trail as it enters the Tenmile Point vicinity. This road also makes a scenic mountain-bike route.

TRAIL NAME: Gemini Bridges. Jun 'au

TRAIL SUMMARY: This trail travels the spectacularly distorted
sandstone maze formed by the Bull and Little canyon systems. It
offers outstanding scenery and provides access to other trails.
This trail is most often biked with a shuttle. See OPTION 1.

TRAIL TYPE: connecting.   OWNERSHIP: BLM

MAP: *Canyon Country* OFF-ROAD VEHICLE TRAIL MAP <u>Island Area</u>.

MILEAGES: 18 miles, 30 miles more if all possible spurs and
loops are taken.

TIME REQUIRED: 4 hours for the Gemini Bridges Trail. Add 3-1/2
hours if the Sevenmile Canyon Rim/Arths Rim/Little Canyon Rim
trail is also taken. Add 6 hours for all the other options.

BEST SEASON: all season trail. The first 4 miles are muddy in
early spring or after extended wet weather.

DIFFICULTY: easy/moderate. The trail steadily loses 900 feet in
elevation. It is mainly packed sand and sediments, and has some
wash sand in Little Canyon.

TECHNICAL RATING: easy, for the main trail and the Four Arches
spur, moderate for the other options.

ACCESS: Drive north from Moab on U.S.191. If shuttling, turn
west through a gate onto a dirt road about 7 miles from the
Colorado River bridge and leave a vehicle here at the lower end
of the trail. To reach the trail head, continue north on U.S.191
to U313, then drive that road toward Dead Horse Point and
Canyonlands National Park. About 0.8 mile beyond the spur road
to Mineral Canyon, the dirt Gemini Bridges trail leaves the
pavement on the left. The trail description begins here, but the
first several miles are usually passable to highway vehicles.

View from near the Gemini Bridges

TRAIL DESCRIPTION:

The trail travels the ridge between two major canyon systems -- Sevenmile on the left, and Bull on the right -- passing spur trails on both sides. At 3.6 miles, keep right at a fork, and about 1/4 mile beyond that, the route goes right at another junction. Highway vehicles should not go beyond this point.

In another mile, the Four Arches Canyon trail spurs right, while the main trail goes left. In about 3/4 mile, turn right on another spur toward the Gemini Bridges. From here it is 1/4 mile through confusing terrain to these large twin natural bridges. At the bridges, note the trail in the Bull Canyon tributary below. This is one optional spur trail. Short hikes to the east and south of the bridges are rewarding.

Back on the main trail, keep left, and in about 1/2 mile and just beyond a short descent, turn left at a minor trail junction and continue for about 1 mile, to the main road. The head of the Sevenmile/Arths/Little Canyon rims trail is 3/4 mile to the left. See OPTION 3. This trail goes right here, and in 3/4 mile comes to a major junction.

Here, this trail goes left. The right trail is the Bull Canyon option. Beyond this junction, the trail passes a short spur trail that provides a broad panoramic view to the south, then descends a steep dugway into Little Canyon. From the base of this grade, it is about 4-3/4 miles to the trail's end. The right spur is the Gold Bar Rim/Little Canyon Loop option.

The main trail goes left, immediately comes to a short spur left to a curious arch, and continues across the sandy wash toward the big "Gooney Bird" monolith. About 1/4 mile beyond the Gooney Bird, another spur enters a side canyon. This spur goes beneath Owl Arch, which is two joined alcoves, then ends at the base of a slender spire called "The Bride." From this trail spur it is about 4 miles to the trail's end at U.S.191.

OPTION 1: Bikers who do not leave a vehicle at the end of the trail, can drive the trail from its head to where the trail first becomes unsafe for highway vehicles, bike from there to the Gemini Bridges and explore Four Arches Canyon, return and drive on down the graded dirt road to the head of the Sevenmile Canyon/Arths Rim Trail, and bike that trail, then continue to the head of the Bull Canyon option trail for additional biking.

OPTION 2: Four Arches Canyon, 4-1/2 miles round trip. This option spurs off the Gemini Bridges Trail, crosses a wash, then follows a power line across Crips Hole and into Four Arches Canyon. As the canyon narrows, there are two jughandle-type arches on the right wall -- Bullwhip and Mosquito -- and two arches high in the left wall of the canyon -- Shadow and Crips -- farther ahead. The last two are difficult to spot.

OPTION 3: The Sevenmile/Arths/Little Canyon rim trail is an 8-1/2-mile, 3-1/2-hour loop. Refer to that trail description.

OPTION 4: Bull Canyon is a 4-1/4 mile round trip. From the trail junction, it travels gradually downward, eventually to reach the Bull Canyon wash-bottom. From there, go down the wash for a short distance to view the pour-off into Day Canyon. The right branch of the wash leads to the spur canyon below the Gemini Bridges. The left enters the Dry Fork of Bull Canyon.

OPTION 5: Gold Bar Rim, 5 miles, the Jeep Arch spur, 4 miles, and the Little Canyon Loop, 5-1/4 miles. To explore these, refer to the appropriate ORV booklet and map.

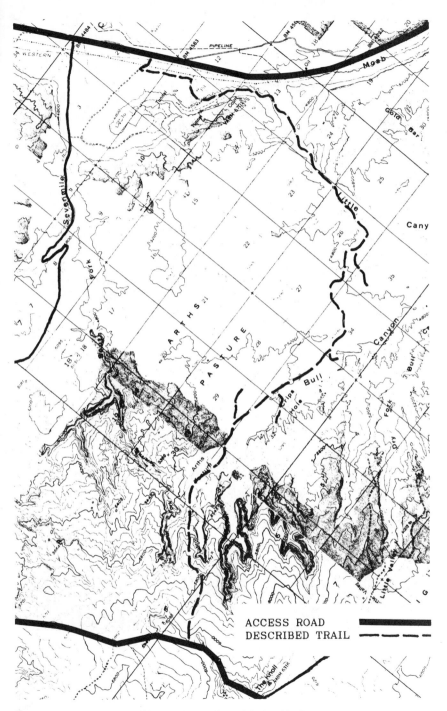

ACCESS ROAD ▬▬▬▬
DESCRIBED TRAIL ▬ ▬ ▬

GEMINI BRIDGES TRAIL MAP

65

Gemini Bridges

TRAIL NAME: Hidden Canyon Rim (The Gymnasium).

TRAIL SUMMARY: This short trail skirts the rims of two lovely hidden canyons and explores an unusual, trail-less slickrock valley. Only two other trails in this book approximate the variety of terrain which The Gymnasium offers. The trail requires use of the navigation pointers earlier in this book.

TRAIL TYPE: spur, as described.   LAND OWNERSHIP: BLM

MAP: *Canyon Country* OFF-ROAD VEHICLE TRAIL MAP Island Area.

MILEAGES: 8 miles round trip, more if Lunar Canyon is explored.

TIME REQUIRED: the trail can be done in 3 hours, but twice that is recommended to allow time for exploring and bike gymnastics.

BEST SEASON: the trail is an all-season trail, but the Blue Hills access road is impassable to highway vehicles after rain.

DIFFICULTY: easy/moderate, with minimal elevation changes. Some sand, but mostly slickrock.

TECHNICAL RATING: easy/moderate, if the trail is followed as described, but can be moderate/technical if used as a "gymnasium." Excellent trail for varying levels of expertise.

ACCESS: The trailhead is 25 minutes from Moab by vehicle. Drive 15 miles north from the Colorado River bridge on U.S.191, then turn left on Blue Hills Road. The trailhead is about 3-1/2 miles from U.S.191, and the trail is described from there.

Hidden Canyon rim

TRAIL DESCRIPTION:

At a trail junction near a corral, turn left then continue, angling right into the small canyon where Brink Spring's water is captured in a water tank. Beyond this tank, the trail climbs steeply past an old log cabin, then levels out on bare slickrock. In about 1/2 mile, the trail swings right and parallels Brink Spring Canyon. The slot canyon that drains into the head of this canyon can be hiked, or used for bicycle gymnastics in places.

In another 1/2 mile, a short spur trail to the right ascends a low slope and gives access to Lunar Canyon, which can be used for further freestyle gymnastics.

The trail continues, paralleling the slickrock-sediment interface on the pebble-strewn slickrock, and is difficult to follow. Watch for occasional cairns. Ahead, as the trail is traveling close to the rim of a shallow canyon on the left, turn left at a junction near the head of that canyon. From this junction, the trail travels a sandy ridge, dips down through a wash, then climbs into a broad expanse of packed dune sand.

Continue generally south, until the trail tops out, then descends a slope of reddish sediments to the rim of Hidden Canyon, with its complex maze of eroded, sloping walls and terraces. The distant La Sals loom above the canyon walls, as shown on this book's wrap-around cover. The slickrock slopes below this rim provide further opportunities for gymnastics.

Brink Spring Canyon

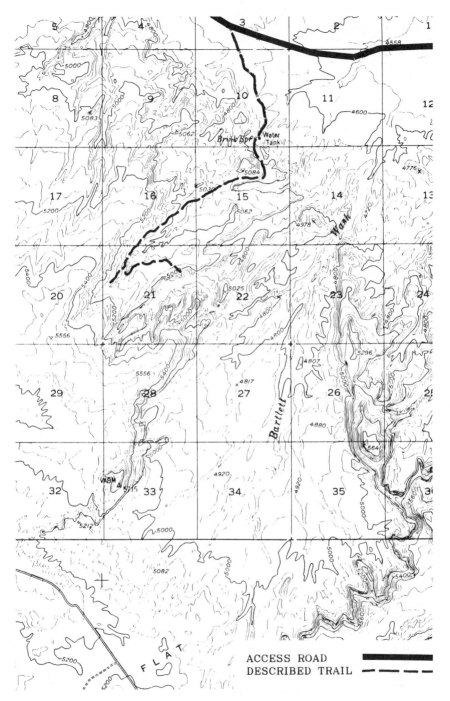

ACCESS ROAD
DESCRIBED TRAIL

HIDDEN CANYON RIM TRAIL MAP

69

Lunar Canyon

TRAIL NAME: Monitor and Merrimac.

TRAIL SUMMARY: This trail offers a wide variety of scenic beauty, including panoramic viewpoints, natural spans, gigantic redrock buttes, mesas and spires, and spring-watered canyons. A loop trail is described, but the entire area is a biking paradise. See the notes at the end of the trail description.

TRAIL TYPE: loop.   LAND OWNERSHIP: BLM

MAP: *Canyon Country* OFF-ROAD VEHICLE TRAIL MAP, Island Area.

MILEAGE: 17 miles for the basic loop.

TIME REQUIRED: 5 hours, days if the entire area is explored.

BEST SEASON: all-season trail, except that snow and rain make parts of the trail slippery. Courthouse Pasture is packed sand that is a serious problem only when very dry.

DIFFICULTY: moderate. The trail surface is packed sand, drift sand, packed sediments, slickrock, and wash bottom. The trail gains 900 feet.

TECHNICAL RATING: moderate.

ACCESS: 15 minutes by vehicle north from Moab. The trailhead is 4.3 miles north of the junction of U.S.191 and U313, just beyond milepost 141. North of the U313/U.S.191 junction, note the high rim to the west, and Corral Canyon beyond the jutting promontory. The route described travels this rim.

Merrimac Butte

71

TRAIL DESCRIPTION:

The trail crosses railroad tracks, then shallow upper Courthouse Wash, before climbing toward the south across rubbly open desert. About 1/2 mile from the highway, turn left at a trail junction, then left again in another 1/2 mile. The trail right comes from Mill Canyon and is the end of the loop.

Just beyond this junction, the trail crosses a wash, where a spur to the right goes to an historic wagon station. The trail continues toward the La Sal mountains, to a fork about 1/2 mile farther on, where the trail climbs steeply to the right toward the base of Courthouse Rock, then passes a huge sand hill that is used for the annual Moab Jeep Safari Sand Hill Climb.

From there, the trail continues along the base of Courthouse Rock, to a broad slickrock terrace on the right, where the Monitor and Merrimac buttes are visible to the south, and the Determination Towers can be seen to the west.

The main trail skirts this slickrock terrace, heading generally toward the Monitor and Merrimac. A little less than a mile beyond the slickrock terrace, just beyond the head of Corral Canyon, watch for a trail that turns left, toward the distant, elevated ridgeline to the east. Beyond this point, it is impossible to give accurate navigational instructions, because the area ahead has been so severely scarred by uranium mining activities. It becomes necessary to freelance navigate a route to the south of Corral Canyon and toward the distant rim.

The trail travels south on or near the rim. Not far beyond the promontory that juts out from the rim, watch for a rock cairn that marks the route down a shallow drainage to Uranium Arch, a large natural span 100 yards or so from the rim. The panorama from anywhere on this rim is outstanding in all directions.

Beyond this spur, the main trail continues to parallel the rim for another 1/2 mile, then leaves the rim, heading in a westerly direction. In another 1/4 mile, the trail reaches the descending white slickrock rim of Sevenmile Canyon. From here, the view to the west is outstanding.

Continue on this trail, skirting along Sevenmile Canyon rim, guided by occasional cairns. After about 3/4 mile, the trail descends toward a tributary of Sevenmile Canyon, heading directly toward the gap between the Monitor and Merrimac. It then turns briefly northward, then westward across Courthouse Pasture.

Again, navigation is freelance, heading in the general direction of the Monitor, the smaller of the two buttes, with the goal being the elevated slickrock terrace between them. It is possible, and an interesting technical challenge, to bike around each of these buttes. Both routes are largely slickrock.

From between the Monitor and Merrimac, the trail heads directly to the north on the broad slickrock terrace between the buttes, toward the Determination Towers. The trail rounds the northern tip of Merrimac Butte, passes a cattle pond blasted into the rock, then continues north across Courthouse Pasture to a trail junction directly east of the Determination Towers.

Take the spur trail west toward the towers. It is easy to reach them as the trail skirts their broad base. The northern tower is the site of a climbing route, "Echo." The popular route is the west face, up to the window at the interface of the Dewey Bridge sandstone and the Entrada slickrock member, then up either side of the window. These towers are known to pilots as the "Kissing Rocks" or "Airport Towers." They are below one of the approaches to the Grand County airport a few miles to the north.

CONTINUED ON PAGE 74

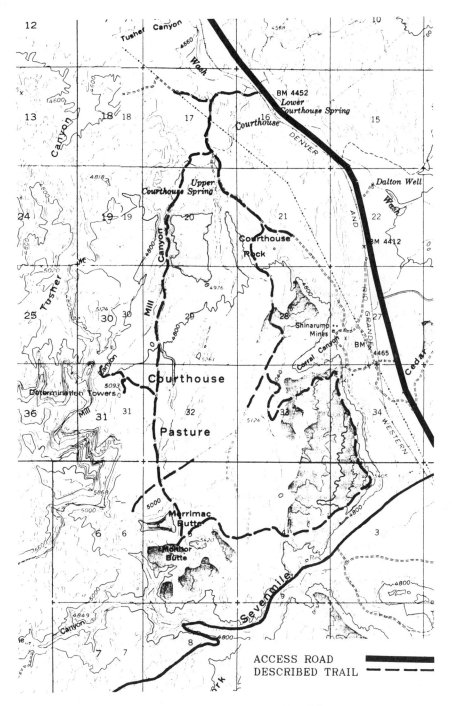

ACCESS ROAD
DESCRIBED TRAIL

MONITOR & MERRIMAC TRAIL MAP

Back on the main trail in Courthouse Pasture, turn north again toward Mill Canyon. From here, the trail gradually descends to the canyon bottom, goes through a fenceline, then shortly angles out to the right past the BLM's "Mill Canyon Dinosaur Trail." About 3/4 mile beyond this point, the trail closes the loop, about a mile from U.S.191.

NOTES:

1. This trail can be biked in one day, but provides access to enough optional loops, spur trails and trail-less slickrock biking for several days of recreation.

2. Navigation in the Courthouse Pasture area depends upon the early identification of its major landmarks and a sense of direction, or a guide familiar with the various routes.

Uranium Arch

Monitor Butte

First mile of Moab Rim trail, viewed from Poison Spider Mesa

Jeep Arch, Poison Spider Mesa

76

TRAIL NAME: Poison Spider Mesa.

TRAIL SUMMARY: This trail climbs onto an elevated mesa that offers spectacular views of the Colorado River gorge, Behind-the-Rocks, the Moab Rim and Moab Valley, Gold Bar Rim, the highlands of Arches National Park, and other more distant features.

TRAIL TYPE: spur.   LAND OWNERSHIP: BLM

MAP: *Canyon Country* OFF-ROAD VEHICLE TRAIL MAP Island Area.

MILEAGE: 14 miles round trip as described, longer if spur trails are explored.

TIME REQUIRED: 5 hours.

BEST SEASON: all-season trail, except when snow is on the ground. Strenuous during dry periods because of sand.

DIFFICULTY: moderate, with a variety of terrain and an elevation gain of 600 feet in the first 3 miles. Strenuous in hot, dry weather. Better after recent rainfall.

TECHNICAL RATING: moderate, with packed sediments, rock ledges, some deep sand, and expanses of bare slickrock.

ACCESS: Trailhead 15 minutes from Moab by vehicle. The trail leaves U279, the Potash Road, 5.8 miles downriver from U.S.191, just before a sign indicating a dinosaur track display.

Rodney Taylor photos

77

TRAIL DESCRIPTION:

The trail starts through a gate, then ascends a steep series of switchbacks, offering excellent views of the Colorado River gorge and an arch in the opposite wall. After about a mile, the trail levels out somewhat. A 1/2-mile hike up a distinct canyon to the right goes to Longbow Arch.

The trail continues parallel to the river gorge for about another mile, bears right and enters a narrow, sandy canyon, then climbs steeply out of the canyon up a series of rocky ledges. After still more climbing, the trail tops out onto a broad level area of slickrock set with pieces of chert darkened with desert varnish, with spectacular views in all directions.

From here, the trail goes generally northeast, crossing a relatively flat expanse of packed sand and low-growing plants. The spur trails encountered should be avoided by bikers, except for one to the right, where the trail starts descending, that goes a few yards on solid rock to a rivergorge rim viewpoint.

As the trail drops down into a sand and slickrock area, navigation becomes difficult without an experienced guide. Watch for cairns, wheel tracks, painted arrows and other clues. Watch also for a pair of painted arrows that indicate a trail fork. The main trail goes left. The right spur goes to Little Arch and excellent views of the river gorge, the portal through which the river leaves Moab Valley, and other familiar features.

The main trail gradually ascends a sandstone dome for a steep 1/2 mile, following painted arrows, and ends near a deep pothole on top of the dome, and a spectacular 360-degree view. From here, bikers may choose to return, or continue for another 1-1/2 miles to where the ORV trail ends at a rim viewpoint. Bikers with the time and energy may choose to further explore the slickrock rimlands of Poison Spider Mesa before returning.

Longbow Arch   Little Arch

78

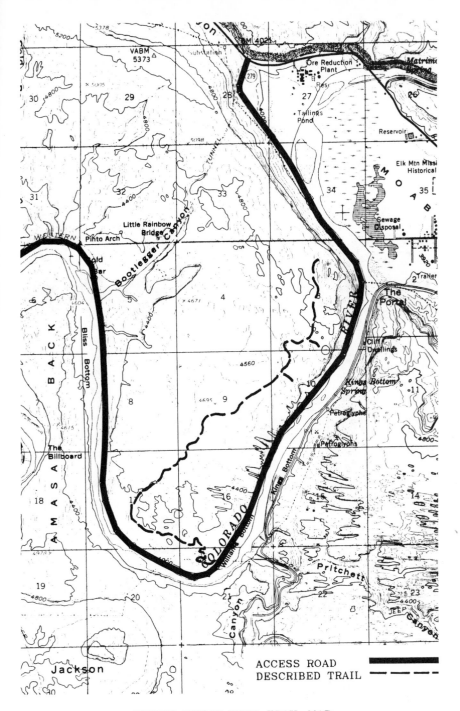

POISON SPIDER MESA TRAIL MAP

Little Canyon Rim viewpoint

TRAIL NAME: Sevenmile Canyon Rim/Arths Rim/Little Canyon Rim.

TRAIL SUMMARY: This trail ascends to lofty Arths Rim, travels that spectacular rim, then descends broad slickrock terraces and Little Canyon Rim to complete a loop. This loop can be combined with the Gemini Bridges trail on a long day.

TRAIL TYPE: loop.   LAND OWNERSHIP: BLM

MAP: *Canyon Country* OFF-ROAD VEHICLE TRAIL MAP Island Area.

MILEAGE: 7 miles round trip.

TIME REQUIRED: 3 hours.

BEST SEASON: all seasons, except when snow is on the ground. Access to the trailhead is muddy following rain or snow-melt.

DIFFICULTY: moderate, with packed drift sand and sediments, slickrock and some loose rubble. The trail gains 700 feet.

TECHNICAL RATING: moderate.

ACCESS: Turn onto the Gemini Bridges Trail from U313. Stay on the graded dirt road for about 6 miles to where a trail goes left. The trail begins here.

Arths Rim   Tom Kuehne photos

TRAIL DESCRIPTION:

From the trailhead, go left, northwest. In 1/3 mile, the spur going right is the return leg of this loop trail. Continue straight, across Arths Pasture, to where the trail goes under some power lines, then turn right on the power-line road.

After about 1-1/4 miles on this road, a spur trail goes left toward the rim of Sevenmile Canyon. The main trail continues past other spurs, staying fairly close to the power line. About 1-3/4 miles along the power-line road, the trail turns right beneath the power line, and in 50 yards comes to a trail fork. Go right here, away from the power lines. Watch for a marked spur left at the base of a small rise. Go left here.

The trail gains the rim in another 1/4 mile. The views from this rim in all directions are outstanding. About 100 yards beyond where the trail rounds a high promontory marked by a stake in a large cairn, the return leg of the trail leaves the rim. This fork may also be marked by cairns. The rim trail continues for about another 1/2 mile, to dead end at the rim of Little Canyon. The trail-less hike to Lin-Lynn Arch begins there.

Leaving the rim, the main trail drops onto slickrock slopes and becomes difficult to find. Watch for tire tracks in soil patches. The trail descends through a slickrock chute that ORV fans call Mirror Gulch, then turns left. Watch for tire tracks and surveyors' ribbons. On bare slickrock, the trail skirts south around the head of a long, deep canyon running to the southwest, then goes between this canyon and a canyon to the left called "Sidepocket."

It skirts another deep canyon immediately on the left, then reaches a broad, descending expanse of slickrock. The trail bears right as it descends this sloping terrace, then reaches packed sediments. The trail on toward the rim of Little Canyon is confused, but almost any route will get there.

Continue downward by any route to the sandy wash of upper Little Canyon. Old mineral-search trails confuse this stretch of the route. Hike down the Little Canyon wash to view its breathtaking, two-step pouroff into the lower canyon. Beyond the wash, the trail ascends rubbly slopes, levels out in sparsely forested, rolling sandflats, then rejoins the first leg of the trail in about 3/4 miles. Turn left to return to the trail head.

Tom Kuehne photo

82

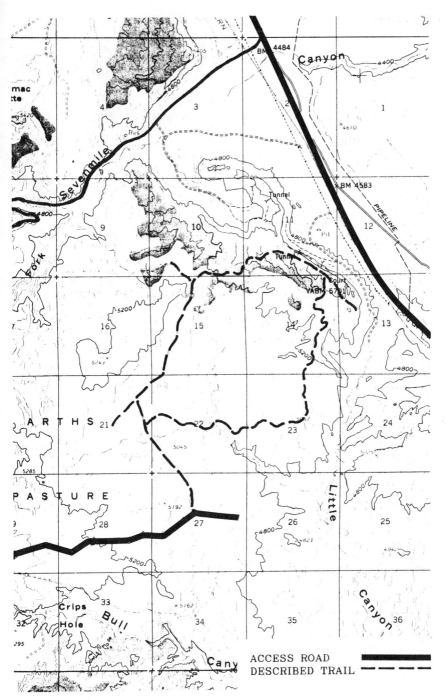

SEVENMILE CANYON RIM/ARTHS RIM/LITTLE CANYON RIM TRAIL MAP

Eric Bajon photo

Shafer Trail

Shafer Trail switchbacks

84

TRAIL NAME: Shafer/Potash. *Cw* *)QY*

TRAIL SUMMARY: This trail begins on the high plateau of the
Island-in-the-Sky district of Canyonlands National Park, descends
to travel the spectacular benchlands of the White Rim trail, then
continues upriver toward Moab through red, intricately-eroded
Cutler sandstone. The trail is described assuming that a shuttle
vehicle has been placed at the end of the paved Potash Road,
U279, or somewhere downriver on its dirt road extension. See
OPTION for another possibility.

TRAIL TYPE: Connecting. OWNERSHIP: 1/2 NPS, 1/2 BLM

MAP: *Canyon Country* OFF-ROAD VEHICLE TRAIL MAP Island Area.

MILEAGES: 26-40 miles, 5 miles more if optional spur is taken.

TIME REQUIRED: 5 hours.

BEST SEASON: all-season, except when snow is on the trail.
The Shafer Trail is slippery when wet.

DIFFICULTY: easy/moderate. The trail loses 1800 feet over its
length, but most of this in the first 5 miles. It is mostly on
packed sediments.

TECHNICAL RATING: easy/moderate.

ACCESS: Park the shuttle vehicle at or beyond the end of U279,
then drive to Canyonlands National Park via U313, which leaves
U.S.191 about 8-1/4 miles north of the Colorado River bridge.
Where the paved road forks left to Dead Horse Point State Park,
continue south. About 1-1/4 miles beyond the Park boundary, turn
left on the Shafer Trail/White Rim road. Park at the day-parking
area 3/4 mile along this road. This is the trailhead.

Potash solar evaporation ponds

85

TRAIL DESCRIPTION:

The trail descends the Shafer Trail switchbacks for the next 5 miles. This trail was first built by cattlemen to move their stock from the pasturelands of the Island-in-the-Sky down to and across the Colorado River, then over Hurrah Pass to Cane Creek Canyon, where they were either wintered or shipped to market. The trail was improved enough to be traveled by 4-wheel-drive vehicles during one of the area's uranium booms, then improved still more to its present condition by the National Park Service when it was included in Canyonlands National Park.

The Shafer Trail ends just beyond the base of the steep grade, where it meets the White Rim and Potash trails at a three-way junction. Turn right here on the White Rim trail, which travels the interface between the White Rim sandstone and reddish Moenkopi sediments, for about 3 miles to Musselman Arch. Just before reaching the short spur trail to this flat-topped natural bridge, a foot trail goes left onto a sandstone peninsula called "The Walking Rocks" by some tour guides. The rest of the White Rim trail is described later in this book.

From the Shafer-White Rim trail junction, the Potash trail immediately descends below the White Rim into dark red Cutler deposits, through which it continues for the balance of the trail. Below Dead Horse Point, the trail travels for some distance on the same rough, gray marine limestone that edges the river bluff along the Hurrah Pass/Chicken Corners trail.

As the trail nears the fenced solar evaporation ponds, an inconspicuous spur to the right goes up a shallow, sandy wash. This 2-1/2 mile spur goes south, then east around the base of Pyramid Butte, to end at an outstanding rim viewpoint.

The main trail continues through the fence, skirts around the evaporation ponds, then descends to lower levels before reaching the potash mill and the end of U279, 19 miles from Moab.

OPTION: The Long Canyon-Shafer Trail Loop (Jughandle Loop). This option is for strong bikers with one vehicle, can be taken in either direction, gains 1800 feet in elevation, and travels largely on packed sediments and pavement. It goes up highly scenic Long Canyon from U279 and Jughandle Arch. From the summit of the canyon grade, the trail continues to U313, takes that road to the junction that heads south toward the Island-in-the-Sky, then takes the Shafer/Potash trail back to Jughandle Arch.

ACCESS ROAD
DESCRIBED TRAIL

SHAFER/POTASH TRAIL MAP

Green River, Stillwater Canyon, White Rim trail

TRAIL NAME: White Rim.

TRAIL SUMMARY: This trail begins and ends on the elevated
peninsular plateau of the Island-in-the-Sky of Canyonlands
National Park. Most of it traverses an intermediate rim of the
Colorado and Green rivers, 1100-1500 feet below the level of the
"Island." The White Rim trail is one of the most scenic trails
in canyon country, and an excellent multi-day bike trail. All
but 26 miles of this trail is in Canyonlands National Park, and
it is well signed by the Park Service and the BLM.

TRAIL TYPE: loop.   LAND OWNERSHIP: BLM and NPS

MAP: *Canyon Country* OFF-ROAD VEHICLE TRAIL MAP Island Area.

MILEAGES: the White Rim Trail loop is 96 miles long. Several
short optional spurs add up to 14 miles more.

TIME REQUIRED: 3-4 days.

BEST SEASON: all-season trail, except when snow is on the trail.
Land slides, wet weather and high river levels occasionally close
the trail, but this is rare. Muddy for long stretches when wet.

DIFFICULTY: moderate. Most of the trail is on relatively flat
packed sand and sediments. Some slickrock, sand and rubble. The
trail loses then regains 1900 feet, most of it on the switchbacks
at either end, the Shafer Trail and the Horsethief Trail.

TECHNICAL RATING: easy/moderate.

ACCESS: 40 minutes from Moab by vehicle. Drive to the Park
Service contact station just beyond the park entrance to the
Island-in-the-Sky district and register. The trail is described
going from east to west, but can be traveled in either direction.

White Rim, aerial view

TRAIL DESCRIPTION:

The first part of this loop route descends the Shafer Trail. At the base of the switchbacks, turn right at the three-way junction onto the White Rim trail. This trail travels much of the way on or near the interface between the White Rim sandstone and the red Moenkopi sediments just above, leaving this interface only when forced to by the terrain.

In 3 miles, the trail comes to the short spur to Musselman Arch, a flat-topped natural bridge in the edge of the White Rim. Farther along, the immense silhouette of The Washerwoman is seen in a projecting Wingate sandstone ridge. Scenic beauty is everywhere, as the trail parallels the vertical ramparts of the Island-in-the-Sky, yet remains high above the Colorado river and its complex of tributary canyons.

The optional spur down Lathrop Canyon is a strenuous 7-mile round trip that drops 400 feet to a campground at river level.

Below Grand View Point, the high southernmost projection of the Island mesa, the trail skirts Monument Basin with its many skyscraper towers of dark red Cutler sandstone. Just beyond Monument Basin, a sandy 2-mile spur trail goes to the White Crack and a camping area. This spur is worth taking for its unique views of the Maze, the Needles, and the complex terrain above the confluence of the Green and Colorado rivers.

Beyond this area, the trail rounds the base of Junction Butte, near the geographical center of Canyonlands National Park, then turns northward, skirting the spectacular tributary gorges of the Green river. The trail then enters the sandy, moderately difficult route up Murphy Hogback, the first of two strenuous humps along this trail, and the approximate halfway mark.

Beyond Murphy Hogback, the trail skirts the rim of the Green River for miles before ascending Hardscrabble Hill, then descending to travel through scenic riverbottoms. The trail crosses the Upheaval Canyon drainage, then passes the spur into the immense Taylor Canyon system. Six miles up this canyon are two popular climbing routes, the spires of Moses and Zeus.

About 2-1/2 miles beyond Taylor Canyon, the trail leaves the park, and in another 4 miles comes to a junction. A spur trail continues upriver to the Mineral Canyon boat launch and Hellroaring Canyon, but the main trail goes right, ascends the steep switchbacks of the Horsethief Trail, then travels 13 miles through rolling pinyon-juniper forestland to end at U313, 8-1/2 miles north of the Park Service contact station.

NOTES:

1. Bike trips on this trail are almost always supported by vehicles, which are needed to carry water and supplies.

2. There are designated campsites at intervals along the trail. The Park Service requires reservations for these, which can be obtained by mail or in person. The popularity of this trail requires that reservations be made well in advance. Write White Rim Reservations, Canyonlands National Park, 125 West 200 South, Moab, Utah 84532.

3. Fires are discouraged by the Park Service, but grates and fire rings are available at the campsites. All firewood must be brought from outside the park.

4. Whether or not campsite reservations have been made, backcountry permits are required before traveling the White Rim. Obtain these at the Island-in-the-Sky contact station.

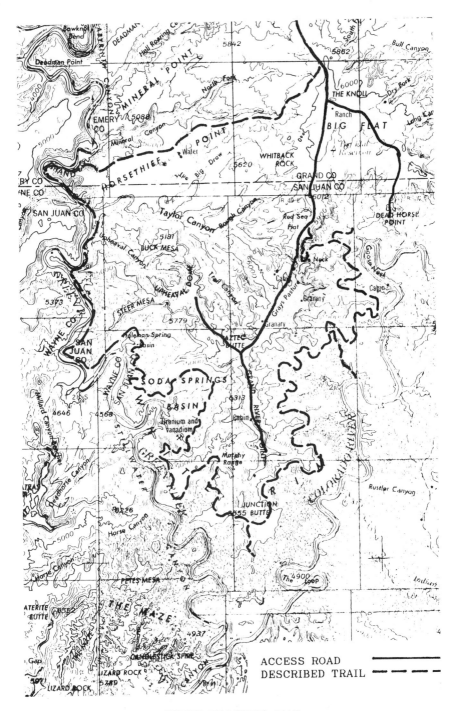

ACCESS ROAD
DESCRIBED TRAIL

WHITE RIM TRAIL MAP

91

Balanced rock, near White Rim trail

The Totem Pole   The White Crack

Green River, Labyrinth Canyon, White Rim trail

LA SALS AREA

AREA TERRAIN

This area is defined by Utah 128 on the northwest, U.S.191 on the west, Utah 46 and Colorado 90 on the south and the Dolores River on the east and northeast. Thus, the La Sals Area includes all of the La Sal Mountains that lie within Utah, plus enough of their foothills in Colorado to include certain access roads, trail junctions and scenic highlights.

The La Sals Area is dominated by the high La Sal Mountains, and this relatively small, isolated range affects the shape of all the terrain within the boundaries of the area. The upper elevations of the mountains are much like other ranges in some respects, with steep, rugged slopes, alpine peaks, small lakes, meadows, streams, woods and mountain wildlife, but the lower slopes are a series of gigantic redrock mesas and benchlands that are cut deeply by wild and rugged canyons, some of them spectacular in size. These great canyons and valleys radiate from the mountains to the Colorado River gorge to the west, and to the Dolores River gorge to the east.

The La Sal Mountains, and their many colorful and magnificent foothill canyons and valleys, plus the mesalands between these lowlands, completely dominate the La Sals Area.

ACCESS ROADS

Access to the La Sals Area from its perimeter highways, Utah 128, U.S.191, Utah 46/Colorado 90 and Colorado 141, is by way of two paved roads, one partly paved road and several graded dirt roads.

Murphy Lane. This paved road begins in Moab, where Mill Creek Drive turns to the south to join U.S.191. Murphy Lane winds along the base of a redrock bluff for several miles, to end at the Moab golf course.

Spanish Valley Road. This paved road goes southeast the length of Moab-Spanish Valley. It begins at Mill Creek Drive in Moab, just south of the Mill Creek Drive-Murphy Lane junction, and ends where the Loop Road and Pack Creek Road join.

Loop Road. This paved road travels the lower slopes of the La Sal Mountains between the end of the Spanish Valley Road and the Castle Valley Road in upper Castle Valley. It provides access to several other roads and off-road vehicle trails.

Pack Creek Road. This partly paved, partly graveled road branches at the junction of the Spanish Valley and Loop roads to go about 3 miles, then end just beyond the Pack Creek picnic grounds.

95

Castle Valley Road. This paved road begins at Utah 128, then travels the length of scenic Castle Valley to end at Castle Creek, where the graded dirt Castleton-Gateway Road begins.

Castleton-Gateway Road. This graded dirt road begins where the Castle Valley Road ends at Castle Creek in upper Castle Valley. It then climbs to travel around the scenic northern flanks of the La Sal Mountains before dropping steeply into the spectacular Dolores River gorge via John Brown Canyon. The road ends by joining Colorado 141 just 1/2 mile south of the town of Gateway.

Entrada Bluffs Road. This graded dirt road begins at Utah 128, where that paved road crosses the Colorado River near the historic Dewey Bridge. It then climbs into higher country to travel near the base of an immense, curving wall of colorful Entrada sandstone. At Cottonwood Canyon, the road crosses the wash. Here, a spur road to the left continues down the canyon to enter a private ranch. The road continues along the base of the bluff but may not be passable to many highway vehicles beyond this junction because of erosion and lack of maintenance. The Entrada Bluffs Road ends at a road-trail junction about 1/4 mile beyond a large terrace left by an oil drilling operation, about 14 miles from Dewey Bridge. The Dolores River Overlook and Thompson Canyon trails begin at this junction. This road makes a good mountain-bike route.

Paradox-Buckeye Road. This steep and rough graded dirt road begins at the town of Paradox, Colorado, climbs out of red walled Paradox Valley toward the west, then follows a circuitous route to Buckeye Reservoir. This road is shown on both Forest Service and U.S.G.S. maps. Two other routes shown on these maps also connect Paradox with Buckeye Reservoir. One goes northward by way of Carpenter Ridge and is normally passable to 2-wheel drive vehicles, but may be in bad condition from lack of maintenance. The third route is strictly 4-wheel-drive.

Canopy Gap Road. This graded dirt road heads north from Utah 46 just east of an old sawmill and about 4 miles east of the town of La Sal. The road goes in a generally northward direction toward Canopy Gap, through the "gap" (a narrow cut in a ridge just beyond a stock pond), then ends at the Geyser Pass trail where that trail closely parallels Geyser Creek. This road makes an easy but scenic mountain-bike route.

Taylor Flat Road. This graded dirt road heads south from the Castleton-Gateway Road about 1 mile east of where that road crosses the Beaver Creek drainage, or about 2 miles east of where the Beaver Basin trail branches from the Castleton-Gateway Road. The Taylor Flat Road travels in a generally southward direction until it ends by joining the Geyser Pass trail. It makes a right turn about midway, in the vicinity of several ranches.

Dolores-San Miguel Confluence Road. This very scenic graded dirt road leaves Colorado 90 just east of Bedrock, Colorado, closely parallels the Dolores River to its confluence with the San Miguel River, then goes up that river gorge to join Colorado 141 just west of Uravan, Colorado. This road provides a picturesque shortcut access route between Colorado 90 and Colorado 141 for those seeking access or egress on the Colorado side of the La Sals Area. This road makes a good mountain-bike route.

Medicine Lake, La Sal Pass

View from the end of Fisher Mesa

TRAIL NAME: Fisher Mesa.

TRAIL SUMMARY: This trail travels the full length of high and beautiful Fisher Mesa, offering breathtaking views at several points along the mesa rim. The view from the tip of Fisher Mesa is outstanding.

TRAIL TYPE: spur.   LAND OWNERSHIP: BLM and USFS

MAP: *Canyon Country* OFF-ROAD VEHICLE TRAIL MAP, <u>Arches</u> & <u>La Sals</u> <u>Areas.</u>

MILEAGE: 18 miles round trip.

TIME REQUIRED: 6 to 8 hours.

BEST SEASON: late spring through fall. Inaccessible otherwise.

DIFFICULTY: moderate/difficult. The trail is on packed sediments, sand, loose rubble, rock ledges and patches of slickrock.

TECHNICAL RATING: moderate/difficult.

ACCESS: Drive 15 miles on U128 from the Colorado River bridge north of Moab to the Castle Valley turnoff. Take the paved Castle Valley road 13 miles to where the pavement ends and the Castleton-Gateway road begins. The Fisher Mesa trail spurs to the left off of this road about 3.7 miles from the pavement.

Fisher Towers, from the end of Fisher Mesa

TRAIL DESCRIPTION:

The trail spurs off of the Castleton-Gateway road, travels out onto a high, wooded point for about 1/4 mile, then angles down a steep slope toward Fisher Mesa proper. At the base of this grade, the trail is only a few feet from the first rim viewpoint. As the trail continues out onto the long, slender mesa, it goes through beautiful woods with plentiful wildlife and unspoiled, picturesque terrain, tiny streams and verdant springs.

Several places along the mesa, the trail swings right to skirt around the upper ends of deeply cut gorges. As it does this, the trail closely approaches the mesa rim, affording outstanding views down into Fisher Valley and beyond.

As the trail nears the mesa tip, it enters a huge devastated area where the lovely pinyon-juniper forest was destroyed many years ago by a "forest management" process called "chaining." Vast windrows of dead trees and disturbed terrain still create navigational and access problems in the area, but the trail does continue to the northwestern tip of Fisher Mesa.

There, the broad panoramic view is breathtakingly beautiful, with Fisher Valley and its enormous "gypsqueeze" on one side and the Onion Creek labyrinth almost directly below. The broad expanse of Richardson Amphitheater and the Colorado River lie to the north and west, Professor Valley, Castle Rock and Adobe Mesa are visible in the southwest, and the La Sal mountains loom to the south. See the Onion Creek trail for additional information about Fisher Valley and Onion Creek.

NOTES:

1. The Castle Valley road passes the classic climb in the region, "Castleton," locally called Castle Rock or Castle Tower. The turnoff to the approach is approximately 4-1/2 miles from U128 on the Castle Valley road. The North Chimney route is a 5.8. An alternate route is a 5.9.

2. This trail can be combined with other trails into several-day hot-weather trips. See OPTIONS suggested from the Onion Creek and Geyser Pass/Gold Basin trails.

Castle Tower, from Fisher Mesa trail

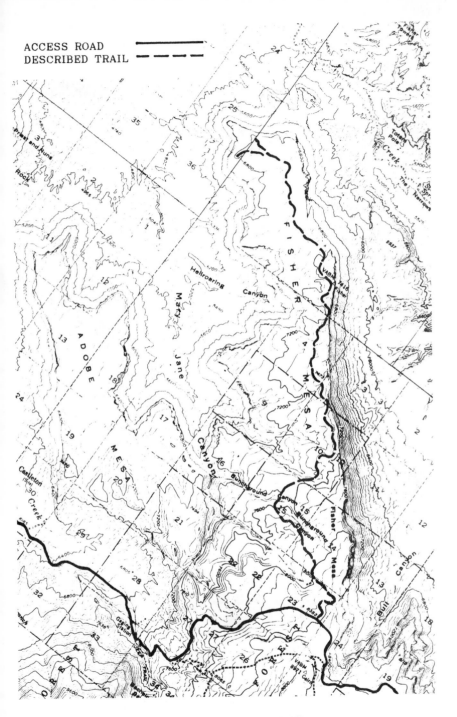

ACCESS ROAD

DESCRIBED TRAIL

FISHER MESA TRAIL MAP

101

Oowah Lake trail

TRAIL NAME: Flat Pass/Mill Creek.

TRAIL SUMMARY: This is a rough, strenuous ride between Mill Creek Canyon and South Mesa, a wild, rugged area close to Moab.

TRAIL TYPE: loop.   LAND OWNERSHIP: BLM

MAP: *Canyon Country* OFF-ROAD VEHICLE TRAIL MAP, <u>Arches & La Sals Areas.</u>

MILEAGES: 19 miles round trip. The first 12 miles are trail, with 7 on pavement through Spanish Valley to close the loop.

TIME REQUIRED: 4 hours.

BEST SEASON: all-season trail, but in the winter may accumulate snow in protected areas, especially in the 1/2-mile stretch from Flat Pass to the Mill Creek crossing.

DIFFICULTY: moderate/strenuous. The trail first gains 200 feet to Flat Pass, then offers 4 miles of rocky ascents and descents. There are also several sandy miles that are strenuous when dry.

TECHNICAL RATING: moderate/technical. The 4 miles after Flat Pass are an unrelenting, jarring technical rollercoaster.

ACCESS: 15 minutes from Moab by vehicle. Drive south on U.S.191 to the Ken's Lake/La Sal Mountain Loop Road turnoff, about 7 miles south of Moab. Follow the Loop Road for 2 miles to the graded gravel turnoff to Ken's Lake to the left. The parking area around Ken's Lake is the trailhead.

Mill Creek Canyon

103

TRAIL DESCRIPTION:

The trail heads toward Flat Pass from Ken's Lake up a graded gravel road, then descends to Mill Creek. There are petroglyphs and historic inscriptions at and beyond the summit of Flat Pass. At the creek, the trail turns right and heads upstream for 1/3 mile to just beyond a small waterfall, where the trail angles left to ford the creek. The rocks in this and other creek-bottom fords are algae-covered and quite slippery.

The trail then ascends a series of broken slickrock ledges and terraces, skirts a picturesque miniature gorge on the right, and heads directly toward South Mesa. For the next several miles, the trail travels between Mill Creek Canyon and the base of lofty South Mesa. Moab-Spanish Valley is to the left, and beyond are the fins of the Moab Rim.

About 2 miles from the creek crossing, the trail dips into a rocky wash, then makes a sharp right up a series of ledges. This wash offers good hiking, with lovely slickrock sculpturing.

The first potentially confusing point on this trail is 3-1/2 miles from the creek crossing, where the trail forks downward from the crest of a hill. Actually, either route is fine. Take the left, which drops into a wash then ascends steeply. The forks rejoin in about 1/4 mile. The trail then passes a fork to the left and in 1/3 mile reaches a T-junction, with South Mesa directly ahead. The trail goes left here, and in another mile climbs very steeply to a fenceline.

For the next 2 miles the trail gradually descends on packed sand. There are several junctions, but the trail goes left each time, down toward Mill Creek and the tilted eastern fractures of the Moab Valley Anticline.

The trail approaches and parallels Mill Creek at creek level, and fords the creek three times before entering the open expanse of Hidden Valley. This is private property, so stay on the trail, which approaches some power poles, then climbs up to the left through a gate, which should be left closed.

About 1/4 mile beyond the gate, the trail arrives at a gravel road, which descends to skirt the county golf course for 1 mile. Turn left at the paved "Canyonlands Circle" to Murphy Lane. Cross Murphy Lane on Spanish Trail Road, and in about 1/2 mile come to Spanish Valley Road. Turn left to Ken's Lake and the trailhead, 6 miles to the south. Turn right to Moab.

NOTE:

This entire route can be biked to and from Moab in a 25-mile loop, of which only about 11 miles is really "trail." This is most safely done from the cemetery in Moab, at the junction of Mill Creek Drive and the Sand Flats Road. Bike south from there on Mill Creek Drive. In 3/4 mile, it forks right, crosses a bridge, then angles left to become Spanish Valley Road. The trailhead at Ken's Lake is 10 miles south. Upon return, turn right at the junction of Spanish Trail Road and Spanish Valley Drive, then return to the cemetery via the outbound route.

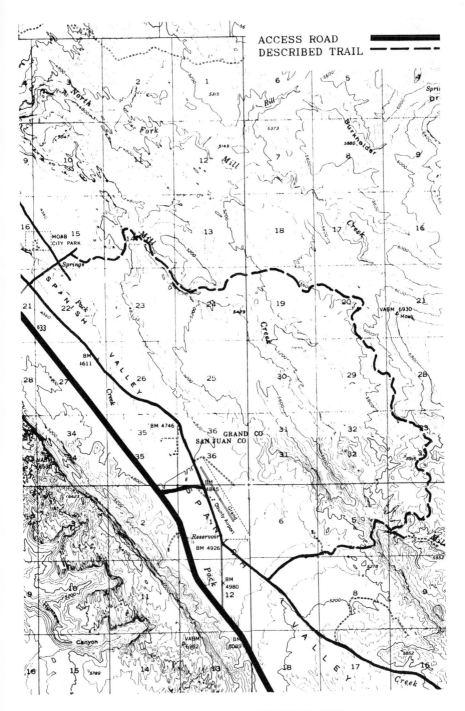

FLAT PASS/MILL CREEK TRAIL MAP

Eric Bajon photo

Mill Creek, near trail ford

TRAIL NAME: Geyser Pass/Gold Basin.

TRAIL SUMMARY: The Geyser Pass trail ascends the steep, aspen-clad western slopes of the La Sal Mountains to 10,600-foot Geyser Pass. The trail to Gold Basin, at the base of Mt. Tukuhnikivatz, is a major spur off of this trail. The trail is signed. It offers cool relief in summer, and is spectacular in early fall. It also has a variety of options.

TRAIL TYPE: connecting and spur.   LAND OWNERSHIP: USFS

MAP: *Canyon Country* OFF-ROAD VEHICLE TRAIL MAP, <u>Arches & La Sals Areas.</u>

MILEAGE: 19 miles round trip.

TIME REQUIRED: 4 hours.

BEST SEASON: late spring through fall.

DIFFICULTY: moderate/strenuous. Most of the trail is graded, packed gravel. It gains 2600 feet to Geyser Pass. The last mile to the summit is rocky, and muddy when wet.

TECHNICAL RATING: easy.

ACCESS: 40 minutes from Moab by vehicle. Drive south from Moab on U.S.191 to the La Sal Loop Road turnoff about 7 miles from Moab. Turn left and stay on the Loop Road to the Geyser Pass road junction, about 12.8 miles from U.S.191 and about 1-1/2 miles before the turnoff to Lake Oowah. This is the trailhead.

TRAIL DESCRIPTION:

The trail climbs through rolling, scrub oak terrain for the first couple of miles, then travels through extensive stands of aspen. The Gold Basin trail spurs right in about 5-1/2 miles. This is a delightful 3-1/2-mile round trip through aspen-conifer forest and across broad meadows to the base of Mt. Tukuhnikivatz.

The main trail continues for 2-1/2 miles more to the Geyser Pass summit. The last mile or so of the trail is very rocky.

OPTION 1. The Geyser Pass trail continues eastward beyond the pass summit to join the Taylor Flat Road. An optional alpine loop, mainly on graded dirt, gravel and asphalt, would be Geyser Pass Trail, Taylor Flat Road, Castleton-Gateway Road, Castle Valley Road, then the Loop Road back to the trailhead. The high point of this loop is 13,600-foot Geyser Pass. The lowest elevation is 6000 feet at the junction of the Castle Valley road and the La Sal Mountain Loop Road.

OPTION 2. Drive to Geyser Pass, then bike back down the 33-mile grade from there to the Loop Road, then down the Sand Flats trail to Moab. This route offers spectacular vistas, and steadily loses 9,500 feet while passing through evergreen, aspen, pinyon-juniper and high-desert life zones. The only significant uphill on this route is the 1-1/2 mile grade beyond Mill Creek.

NOTES:

1. The non-technical ascent of Mt. Tukuhnikivatz, then along a saddle to Mt. Peale, the highest in the La Sals, is a popular day trek. The peak can also be reached from Gold Basin, but the most popular route is from La Sal Pass.

2. Gold Basin is a popular cross-country ski area, but access is sometimes a problem. The elevation at the Geyser Pass trailhead is 8000 feet.

3. This trail is only one of many that branch from the La Sal Mountain Loop Road. Others are listed in the charts later in this book. All are mountain roads that gain elevation to their various destinations, whether passes, lakes, or basins. Most are signed by the Forest Service.

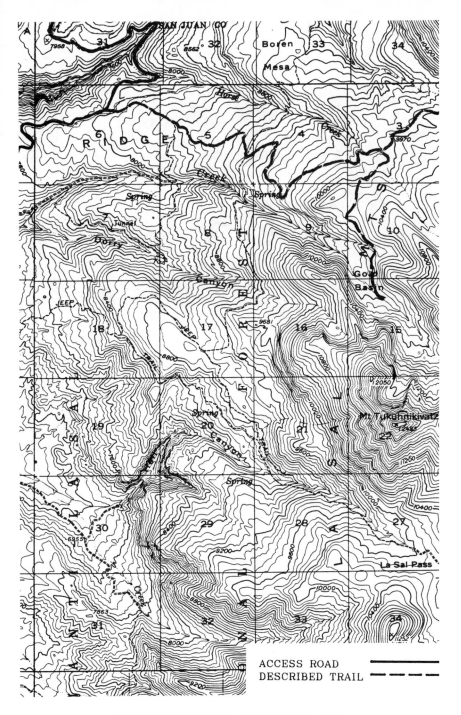

GEYSER PASS/GOLD BASIN TRAIL MAP

Onion Creek trail

TRAIL NAME: Onion Creek.

TRAIL SUMMARY: This colorful and unique trail closely parallels
the twisting course of odorous Onion Creek through a maze of dark
red Moenkopi and Cutler sediments, and through an upthrust of
gypsum. Lower Onion Creek winds through a maze of weirdly eroded
rock, colorfully banded minerals and echoing grottoes. The trail
ends in upper Fisher Valley at the junction of two other trails.

TRAIL TYPE: connecting.   LAND OWNERSHIP: BLM

MAP: *Canyon Country* OFF-ROAD VEHICLE TRAIL MAP, <u>Arches & La Sals</u>
      <u>Areas.</u>

MILEAGE: 19 miles, longer if spurs are taken.

TIME REQUIRED: 3 hours, as described.

BEST SEASON: all-season trail, but the last 6 miles may be
difficult in the winter or when wet.

DIFFICULTY: easy/moderate. The trail surface is packed, and is
maintained to provide access to a private ranch in upper Fisher
Valley. The trail gains 1200 feet along its length, but this is
a factor only on the 2-mile, 600-foot climb near the trail's end.

TECHNICAL RATING: easy.

ACCESS: The trail leaves U128, "The River Road," between mile
posts 20 and 21. This is 4-1/2 miles beyond the Castle Valley
turnoff when driving from Moab, and 3/4 mile beyond the Fisher
Towers turnoff when driving from Cisco and Dewey. There is a
sign at the trailhead: "Taylor Livestock, Fisher Valley Ranch."

Tom Kuehne photos

111

TRAIL DESCRIPTION:

The trail winds through low-lying rock-gardens of red sandstone, crossing Onion Creek numerous times. The creek usually runs clear, but is highly mineralized, malodorous and not potable, even with treatment.

After 3-1/2 miles, the trail reaches the Onion Creek narrows and climbs temporarily above the creek. It is possible to bike through the narrows, if care is taken to watch for soft spots. The narrows route rejoins the vehicle trail in about 3/4 mile.

Meanwhile, the trail travels terraces above the creek, crossing it at one point on a bridge, then rejoins it to continue through more red sandstone formations before entering a maze of whitish, crystalline gypsum hills.

The trail comes to Stinking Spring about 6 miles from the trailhead. This vegetated, malodorous seep marks a sandy side-canyon to the left that goes to an old mine and a deep grotto.

The trail continues to parallel Onion Creek and, about 1 mile beyond Stinking Spring, begins a winding ascent that tops out in elevated Fisher Valley at a junction, where this trail ends. The left fork is the Cottonwood Canyon trail. The trail straight ahead is the Thompson Canyon trail.

OPTION: With a shuttle to the Polar Mesa trailhead, the Onion Creek trail can be the last half of a 26-mile "coast," or it can be the last leg of a 50-mile loop, via Castle Valley, the Castleton-Gateway road, the Polar Mesa trail, the Thompson Canyon trail, then down Onion Creek, with optional spurs along the way.

NOTES:

1. Fisher Valley is one of eight "salt valleys" around the La Sal Mountains. These valleys are anticlines formed by upthrusting ridges of deep Paradox Formation salts, with the centers of these anticlines eroded into valleys.

2. In contrast to the neglect suffered by other county routes, the "maintenance" this trail receives is often so enthusiastic that fresh bulldozer work sometimes makes it difficult for bikes to travel, even through the narrows.

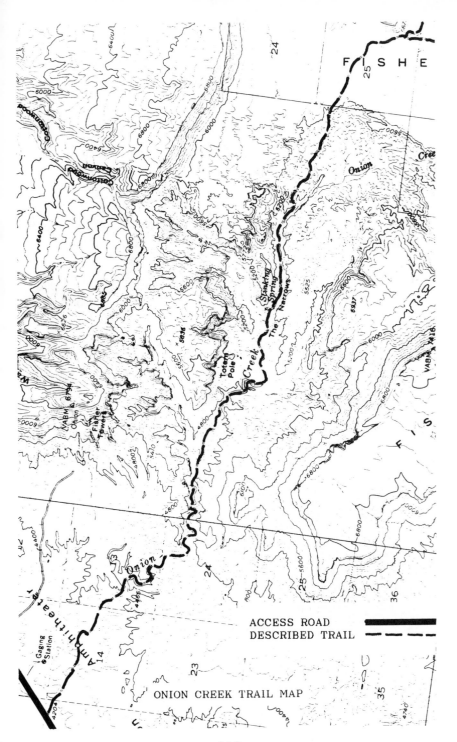

ACCESS ROAD
DESCRIBED TRAIL

ONION CREEK TRAIL MAP

Castle Valley, from Porcupine Rim trail

TRAIL NAME: Porcupine Rim.

TRAIL SUMMARY: This trail skirts around upper Negro Bill Canyon, then travels breathtaking Porcupine Rim above Castle Valley. It offers access to several spur trails in the isolated slickrock maze between Porcupine Rim and Negro Bill Canyon.

TRAIL TYPE: spur.   LAND OWNERSHIP: BLM

MAP: *Canyon Country* OFF-ROAD VEHICLE TRAIL MAP, <u>Arches & La Sals Areas.</u>

MILEAGE: 14 miles, longer if spur trails are explored.

TIME REQUIRED: 6 hours, longer if spur trails are explored.

BEST SEASON: 3-season trail. Snow makes the first few miles impassable, even in milder winters.

DIFFICULTY: moderate/strenuous. The trail gains 700 feet in the first 3 miles, loses 600 feet, then goes back up again.

TECHNICAL RATING: moderate/technical. The trail travels broken slickrock, ledges, and packed sediments and drift sand.

ACCESS: 20 minutes from Moab by vehicle. Drive or bike on the Sand Flats Road past the Moab Slickrock Bike Trail to where the road is on a ridge between two canyon systems, with Negro Bill on the left and Rill on the right. At a water tank there, the lower trailhead goes through a gate on the left. Optionally, if you have a 4-wheel-drive shuttle, continue on the Sand Flats Road about 1-1/2 miles to the upper trailhead, which goes through a fenceline on the left.

Eric Bajon photo

115

TRAIL DESCRIPTION:

From the lower trailhead at the tank, the trail skirts upper Negro Bill Canyon on narrow terraces to its junction with the upper trailhead, which comes in from the right.

From the upper trailhead, the trail goes through the fence, then descends steeply to the slopes above upper Negro Bill Canyon, where it joins the trail from the lower trailhead.

From this junction, the trail continues along the terraced slope, then descends to cross the shallow upper wash of Negro Bill Canyon. It then climbs steeply toward Porcupine Rim, which is the southwestern rim of Castle Valley. For the next 1-1/2 miles, the trail closely parallels the rim, providing excellent views of Castle Valley. Round Mountain is directly below.

The next described part of this trail is a rather strenuous spur that descends about 600 feet from Porcupine Rim to the base of Coffee Pot Rock, then returns.

About 1/2 mile from where the trail leaves the rim, continue straight through a 4-way junction, and in another 1/3 mile, turn left again. Take the trail to the right here when returning. The trail continues around the base of Coffee Pot Rock, to end at a magnificent panorama. On the return trip, go left at the first junction beyond Coffee Pot Rock for 1/3 mile to another junction.

At this point, going right, or eastward, toward Porcupine Rim is the return route. Optionally, go left around Coffee Pot Rock. This spur trail ends about 4 miles beyond this promontory, at the head of Drinks Canyon, where a short hike along its rim goes to a spectacular view of the Colorado River gorge. A spur trail from here continues to and beyond Jackass Canyon.

NOTES:

1. The Porcupine Rim area has many more trail spurs than were described, making navigation difficult. Use of the map listed is essential to staying on the described trail.

2. Another spur trail goes to the end of Mat Martin Point, but this trail is difficult to find and follow without a knowledgeable guide.

Eric Bajon photo

116

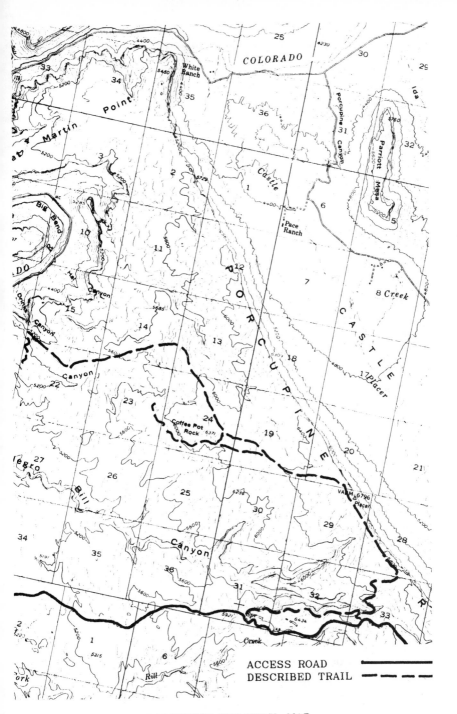

ACCESS ROAD ━━━━━
DESCRIBED TRAIL ━ ━ ━

PORCUPINE RIM TRAIL MAP

117

MAZE AREA

AREA TERRAIN

The Maze Area is defined by the Green-Colorado rivers on the east, the Wayne-Emery county line on the north, the Hans Flat Road on the west, and its extension to beyond the head of the Flint Trail switchbacks.

The western part of this area is largely open desert, with the northern part cut by occasional relatively shallow washes and sandstone canyons. The southern part is slashed by the upper ends of several major and spectacular canyon systems.

This desert area ends at a series of rimlands that overlook the gigantic stone labyrinth that gave the Maze Area its name. There, far below the rimlands, an incredibly complex maze of canyons cut into ancient rock made up of red-banded seashore sands extends eastward to the inner gorges of the Green and Colorado rivers. Between the rimlands and this natural maze, painted-desert deposits add their muted hues to the scene.

ACCESS ROADS

All highway vehicle access into the Maze Area from its perimeter road, Utah 24, is via the Hans Flat Road.

Hans Flat Road. This graded dirt road heads east from Utah 24 a short distance south of the junction where a paved road heads toward Goblin Valley State Park. It crosses open desert for about 46 miles, to Hans Flat, where a National Park Service ranger station serves as a contact point for Maze Area visitors. Inquire there about the condition of the road beyond this point.

Other access roads. There are two other routes into the Maze area, but neither can reliably be used by highway vehicles. Bikers with 4-wheel-drive vehicles may choose to approach the Maze area from a road that goes south from the town of Green River, or one that goes northeastward from where Utah 95 crosses upper Lake Powell, but both routes are long, go through remote terrain, are infrequently traveled, are sporadically maintained, and are subject to severe damage from precipitation.

INTRODUCTION

Biking in the Maze area presents unique problems. It is very remote from all sources of supplies, services and other traveler amenities. All food, water, vehicle fuel and other expendable supplies must be taken into the Maze. There are no sources for supplies or services nearer than the small towns of Green River and Hanksville, although limited emergency help is generally available at the Hans Flat ranger station.

Thus, those who wish to use bicycles to sample the many miles of ORV trails in the general Maze area must first drive to the ranger station, where backcountry permits are issued for those who wish to enter Canyonlands National Park, either the Maze or the Horseshoe Canyon annex, and take with them all the water and other supplies needed for their anticipated stay.

The stair-step nature of Maze area topography presents an additional problem for those driving 2-wheel-drive highway vehicles. Only the higher level is accessible to such vehicles.

There are essentially three levels in the area. The highest of these ranges from 6,000 to 7,000 feet in elevation. In this level are Hans Flat, Land's End, The Big Ridge, Panorama Point and Cleopatra's Chair.

The next level ranges from 5,000 to 6,000 feet, the level traveled by the Maze Overlook and Land of Standing Rocks trails and several others. The lowest level ranges from 4,000 to 5,000, the level of the Green River and the lower canyon-bottoms, including those in The Maze. Only the extremely remote Anderson Bottom/Queen Ann Bottom trail descends this low, but there are many good hiking routes in this level.

The uppermost of these three levels is generally open to highway vehicles for the warmer three seasons. The lower levels may be open to 4-wheel-drive vehicles even in the winter, when any of the three access roads is passable.

Although the practical problems associated with mountain biking in the Maze area require more than casual planning, the unique nature of the area makes the additional effort and inconvenience worthwhile.

The Maze

TRAIL NAME: Flint/Land of Standing Rocks.

TRAIL SUMMARY: This marked trail descends the steep, rough switchbacks of the Flint Trail, then travels an intermediate rim at the base of the Orange Cliffs for several miles, offering views of Ernies Country and the distant Needles district of Canyonlands National Park. The trail then descends to travel through desert pastures and slickrock for several miles before entering the Land of Standing Rocks, the lofty ridge between The Maze and The Fins. The trail ends on cliffs high above the Colorado River in a sandstone fairyland called The Doll House.

TRAIL TYPE: spur.   LAND OWNERSHIP: NPS

MAP: *Canyon Country* OFF-ROAD VEHICLE TRAIL MAP, <u>Maze Area.</u>

MILEAGE: 64 miles round trip, more if spur trails are explored.

TIME REQUIRED: 3 days.

BEST SEASON: 3-season trail. The access road and higher elevations of the trail receive snowfall in the winter.

DIFFICULTY: moderate. The trail surface is largely slickrock or packed sediments and drift sand. The last 3 miles are sand that may be a problem when dry. The trail loses 1,600 feet, then regains it upon return. Much of this elevation change is in two short, steep stretches, with most of the trail relatively flat.

TECHNICAL RATING: easy/moderate.

ACCESS: Drive 46 miles from U24 to the Hans Flat ranger station. After obtaining the required backcountry permit and checking current trail conditions with the ranger on duty, continue about 13 miles beyond the ranger station to the head of the Flint Trail. The road is generally passable this far to highway vehicles, and sometimes beyond to Lands End and The Big Ridge.

TRAIL DESCRIPTION:

The trail descends the Flint Trail switchbacks to Flint
Cove, where it winds for 2 miles to a junction. At the junction,
an optional spur left goes to the Golden Stairs hiking trail and
the Maze Overlook. The main trail goes right (south), to wind
along the base of the Orange Cliffs.

About 3-1/2 miles from the Maze Overlook junction, the trail
angles down into the open country of Waterhole Flat to an easily
missed junction west of a promontory called Teapot Rock. The
trail to the south here goes toward the Sunset Pass spur trail
and reaches U95 and upper Lake Powell in about 30 miles. This
trail goes left and swings east then north around Teapot Rock and
the rough slickrock ledges of upper Teapot Canyon.

Beyond Teapot Canyon, the trail meets no more junctions
until just beyond Lizard Rock, another outstanding promontory.
There, a spur loop goes to Chimney Rock, a tall sandstone spire.
From here on to its end, the main trail is sandy. The loop
avoids some sand, but also bypasses one primitive campsite.

Both the main trail and the loop trail continue to The Doll
House and the end of the vehicle trail, where the upper end of
the foot trail down to Spanish Bottom and the river begins.

NOTES:

1. The support of a 4-wheel-drive vehicle is recommended
for biking this and other trails in the lower levels of the
Maze area, for carrying supplies, for carrying bicycles over
the rougher stretches, and for use as a base camp.

2. Bikers who wish to take this and other trails
unsupported by a vehicle, can bike-pack and explore from a
base at one of the several designated campsites, although
carrying enough water can be a problem in warmer weather.

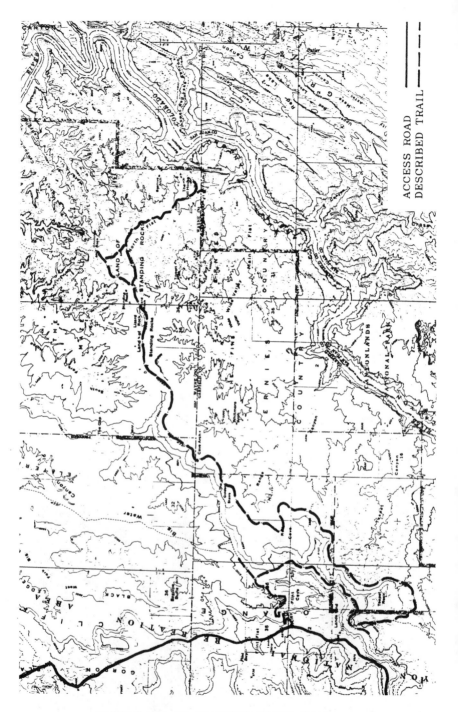

ACCESS ROAD

DESCRIBED TRAIL

FLINT/LAND OF STANDING ROCKS TRAIL MAP

NEEDLES AREA

AREA TERRAIN

The Needles Area is defined by Utah 211 and lower Indian Creek Canyon on the north, the Colorado River on the west, the northeastern boundary of the Dark Canyon Primitive Area and the Abajo Mountains on the south, and U.S.191 on the east. This area includes the Needles District of Canyonlands National Park.

Most of the Needles Area is a vast expanse of colorful, ancient sandstone that has been eroded into a maze-like complex of sandstone canyons, spires, domes, fins, ridges, arches, caves and other landforms. As this unique area blends into the Abajo Mountains foothills, the canyon-slashed highlands there are a second type of terrain within the area. The entire Needles Area is known for its many spectacular natural arches, its park-like meadows surrounded by walls of color-banded spires, or "needles," and its hundreds of fascinating archeological sites. The extreme eastern end, in the vicinity of U.S.191, is relatively open, rolling desert studded with eroded sandstone outcroppings.

ACCESS ROADS

All access into the Needles Area is from its perimeter road, Utah 211, or from U. S. Forest Service roads that approach the area from the Abajo Mountains to the south. All vehicle trails described in this area begin from Utah 211 or its extension into Canyonlands National Park, or spur from another trail.

INTRODUCTION

Of the six geographic areas identified in this book, four include areas administered by the National Park Service. Of these, the Needles area has some of the most remarkable scenery in the southwest, but many of the trails are very sandy. The Park Service actively discourages biking in Lavender, Davis, Salt and Horse canyons. In addition to the trails described in this book, the Harts Point and Lockhart Basin trails offer bikers relatively easy yet spectacular routes to explore. These are described in another *Canyon Country* book. See the trail charts in the next chapter, and FURTHER READING at the end of the book.

Colorado River Overlook

TRAIL NAME: Colorado River Overlook.

TRAIL SUMMARY: This trail goes to the Lower Jump of Salt Creek, then continues to a rim viewpoint overlooking the confluence of lower Salt Creek Canyon and the Colorado River gorge.

TRAIL TYPE: spur.   LAND OWNERSHIP: NPS

MAP: *Canyon Country* OFF-ROAD VEHICLE TRAIL MAP, Canyon Rims & Needles Areas.

MILEAGES: 14 miles round trip, 3-1/2 miles more if the optional spur is taken.

TIME REQUIRED: 2-1/2 hours.

BEST SEASON: all-season trail.

DIFFICULTY: easy/moderate.   The trail surface is largely packed sediments, with 2-1/2 miles of wash sand along lower Salt Creek. The difficulty of the trail there is affected by recent vehicle traffic.   There is little elevation change on this trail.

TECHNICAL RATING: easy for 6 miles, moderate for the last mile.

ACCESS: The trail leaves the pavement in Canyonlands National Park at the Park Service contact station.

Colorado River Overlook

TRAIL DESCRIPTION:

The trail first goes through open meadows dotted with low Cedar Mesa sandstone monoliths, then heads directly for distant Junction Butte, the approximate geographic center of the park.

In 2-3/4 miles, the trail crosses Salt Creek, about 250 yards upwash of the Lower Jump. This "jump," or sudden drop, is quite picturesque when water is flowing in the creek.

About 1-1/2 miles beyond the creek crossing, the trail goes left at a junction, where an optional spur ends at a fence in about 1-3/4 miles. The main trail continues toward the overlook, ultimately gaining a high ridge between lower Salt Creek Canyon and the Colorado River gorge. The last mile of the trail is rough and moderately technical as it traverses knobby slickrock.

From the trail end, it is necessary to walk the remaining few yards to the viewpoint. The panorama there is outstanding. Below, Salt Creek winds through deep and narrow goosenecks toward its confluence with the Colorado. Junction Butte is due north. From there, clockwise, are Grand View Point, the southernmost tip of Island-in-the-Sky, and below that the white-topped spires of Monument Basin. The ramparts of Island-in-the-Sky extend northeast to Dead Horse Point. Across the Colorado River gorge, the cliffs of Hatch Point indicate the Canyon Rims Recreation Area, with the peaks of the La Sal Mountains beyond.

On around the horizon are upper Indian Creek Canyon, the Six-shooter Peaks, Molly's Nipple, the Abajo Mountains, lofty Cathedral Butte, the highlands of the Wooden Shoe buttes, the spires and pinnacles of the Needles, the Standing Rocks, the Orange Cliffs, Elaterite Butte, and Ecker Butte.

The first published description of this magnificent view was written by John Strong Newberry, physician and general scientist with the 1859 Macomb Expedition. The members of this American mapping expedition were the first white people to see the area now largely protected within Canyonlands National Park. A second, unpublished description by Charles Dimmock, the expedition's surveyor, was recently found in federal archives. The story of this little-known expedition is described in the book CANYONLANDS NATIONAL PARK - Early History and First Descriptions, listed under FURTHER READING.

NOTE: Bighorn sheep are sometimes seen near this trail.

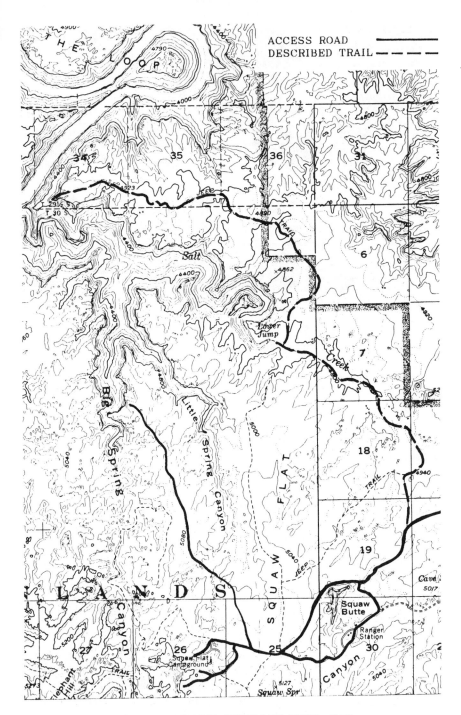

ACCESS ROAD

DESCRIBED TRAIL

COLORADO RIVER OVERLOOK TRAIL MAP

Cliff dwellings in Beef Basin Wash

Upper Salt Creek Canyon, from Big Pocket Overlook

TRAIL NAME: Cottonwood Canyon/Beef Basin/Bobbys Hole-Ruin Park.

TRAIL SUMMARY: This trail begins at Dugout Ranch south of
Canyonlands National Park and skirts the eastern base of Bridger
Jack Mesa to looming Cathedral Butte, with a side trip to Big
Pocket Overlook. The trail climbs forested highlands, then
descends to go through a series of open meadowed areas, or
"parks," in which prehistoric Anasazi ruins are found.
    Beyond the parks, the trail descends steeply into the
magnificent "grabens" of the Needles area of the park, then
continues to challenging Elephant Hill. In scenic values,
archeological interest, and variety of biking terrain, this trail
is unsurpassed.
    The trail should be done with 4-wheel-drive support, but is
made possible unsupported by springs in Beef Basin.

TRAIL TYPE: connecting loop.   LAND OWNERSHIP: BLM, NPS, USFS

MAP: *Canyon Country* OFF-ROAD VEHICLE TRAIL MAP, Canyon Rims &
    Needles Areas.

MILEAGES: 54 miles for the described loop, add for spurs taken.

TIME REQUIRED: 3 days.

BEST SEASON: three-season trail, muddy in spring. Snow makes
the highlands around Cathedral Butte, Boundary Butte and Horse
Mountain inaccessible from November through April. The alternate
approach via Elk Ridge from Blanding is also closed then.

DIFFICULTY: moderate. The trail surface is packed sediments and
drift sand. The sandy stretches are difficult during dry
weather. The trail gains 1,700 feet in the 15 miles between
Dugout Ranch and Cathedral Butte, then gains an additional 1,000
feet in the 7 miles from Cathedral Butte to the base of Horse
Mountain, where the elevation is 8,000 feet. Most of this
elevation gain is lost between Horse Mountain and Bobbys Hole.

TECHNICAL RATING: easy/moderate. There are some technical
stretches along this trail, notably around Bobbys Hole, in Beef
Basin, and on the Elephant Hill trail.

ACCESS: This trail leaves U211 at the Dugout Ranch turn-off,
about 8 miles beyond Newspaper Rock, and about 13 miles east of
the boundary of Canyonlands National Park. Parking is not
allowed on the private property at the trailhead, but a shuttle
vehicle can be parked with prior permission at the small resort
at the park entrance, or beside the various roads east of U211.

TRAIL DESCRIPTION:

About 3-1/2 miles from the Dugout Ranch trailhead, the Cottonwood Canyon segment of the trail forks right, fords a small creek, then climbs onto the rocky, sparsely-forested terraces along the base of Bridger Jack Mesa. Lofty Cathedral Butte, distinctively crested on top with a knob and a narrow pinnacle, is visible after about 10 miles.

At about 14 miles, a short spur to the right leads to a viewpoint above upper Lavender Canyon. About 15-1/2 miles from the trailhead, the Big Pocket Overlook spur trail goes right at the base of Cathedral Butte. This rough 5-mile round trip goes to outstanding viewpoints overlooking upper Salt Creek Canyon, one of its tributaries, Big Pocket, and upper Lavender Canyon.

Beyond this junction, the route described is shown on the referenced map as the "Beef Basin Trail." In 3/4 mile, the trail passes the parking area and trailhead of the foot trail down into upper Salt Creek Canyon.

The trail climbs for the next several miles to the base of Horse Mountain, offering views of upper Salt Creek Canyon. About 8 miles beyond Cathedral Butte, it turns right from the graded road and descends toward Beef Basin and the other nearby parks. About 2 miles after the trail enters the first of these, House Park, it reaches a trail junction and register.

Here, the main route, called the Bobbys Hole-Ruin Park trail on the map, goes right. The trail left climbs a low ridge, then drops into Beef Basin. A loop trail circumnavigates this scenic basin, with spur trails along the way to camping sites and various prehistoric ruins. There is a perennial spring on the eastern side of Beef Basin, but the water should be treated.

The Beef Basin loop is primarily on packed sediments, but has several sandy stretches, as do both of the major spurs off of the Beef Basin loop. This optional loop is recommended for bikers with time, stamina, and interest in archeological sites.

The main trail continues northward from the trail register, then drops into Middle Park and Ruin Park. This area contains many remnants of the prehistoric Anasazi culture. Now, the climate is semi-arid and the dominant vegetation is sage, but earlier a wetter climate permitted the farming of these parks.

There are spurs leading from the main trail to archeological structures. These receive little practical protection, so please respect their fragile nature. Avoid camping near ruins.

From Ruin Park, the trail winds through the narrow meadow of Pappys Pasture, then descends a very steep grade into Bobbys Hole. The trail travels the length of this extensive canyon system, then crosses Butler Wash and Butler Flat as it approaches Chesler Canyon. The scenic beauty in this area is outstanding.

There is a short spur to Horsehoof Arch and a small group-camping area about 4 miles past the park boundary. Just beyond this spur, there is a small designated camping area.

Where the trail reaches a junction in Chesler Canyon, the head of the unique Joint Trail hiking route into Chesler Park is a short distance upcanyon. From this junction it is about 3 miles to where this trail connects with the Elephant Hill trail. Refer to the description of that trail beyond this junction.

OPTION: Up Cottonwood Canyon and to the tip of Big Pocket Overlook and back makes an excellent 36-mile round trip.

CONTINUED ON PAGE 132

130

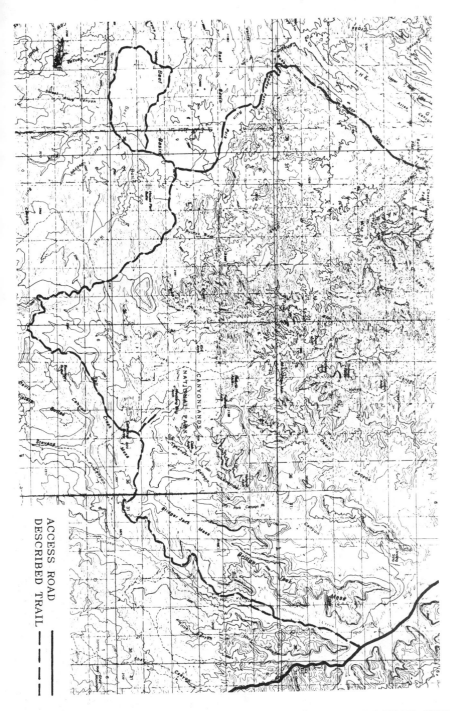

ACCESS ROAD ⸻

DESCRIBED TRAIL ⸺ ⸺ ⸺

COTTONWOOD CANYON/BEEF BASIN/BOBBYS HOLE-RUIN PARK TRAIL MAP

NOTES:

1. This trail can be taken in either direction, but is
described to enable support vehicles to go down, rather than
up, the very rough and steep grade between Bobbys Hole and
Pappys Pasture. Support vehicles must be low-geared, high-
clearance 4-wheel-drive, and driven by experienced drivers.

2. After the trail enters the park, camping may not be
available, particularly on weekends. There are only three
small designated camping areas between the park boundary and
Elephant Hill. Backcountry permits for these must be
procured in advance at the park contact station.

3. Lavender Canyon was named after an early rancher in this
area. See *One Man's West*, by David Lavender.

Pioneer cabin, near Beef Basin

Hiking the Joint Trail

Elephant Hill

Tom Kuehne photo

TRAIL NAME: Elephant Hill.

TRAIL SUMMARY: This trail, with its several spurs, offers biking access to many unique and beautiful highlights within the Needles District of Canyonlands National Park, and also provides access to several outstanding hiking and connecting trails.

TRAIL TYPE: connecting loop.   **LAND OWNERSHIP:** NPS

MAP: *Canyon Country* OFF-ROAD VEHICLE TRAIL MAP, Canyon Rims & Needles Areas.

MILEAGE: basic loop 8.5 miles, more if spurs are taken.

TIME REQUIRED: 2 hours for the loop, more if spurs are taken.

BEST SEASON: all-season trail. Elephant Hill and other sections of this trail may accumulate snow and ice in the winter. Then, the trail is closed to vehicles, but bikers can usually portage.

DIFFICULTY: moderate to strenuous. The amount of sand on the trail dictates a "moderate" rating regardless of other factors.

TECHNICAL RATING: moderate. There are slickrock ledges at many points along this trail.

ACCESS: In the Needles district of Canyonlands National Park, drive or bike the dirt road to the base of Elephant Hill. There is a parking lot, picnic area, and pit toilet at the trailhead.

Glen Lathrop photos

135

TRAIL DESCRIPTION:

The trail immediately ascends the steep slickrock slopes and ledges of Elephant Hill. After it tops out at a magnificent viewpoint, the trail crosses Elephant Hill then descends a grade even more technical than the ascent. There is no general agreement about the origin of the name, "Elephant Hill."

The trail next winds for a short distance through lower Elephant Canyon then turns left into Devils Kitchen. At the Devils Pocket, a designated camping area, the trail reaches a junction. The magnificent spires and towers visible along this stretch of the trail eroded from Cedar Mesa sandstone. Similar but less delicate spires are found in other sections of the park and in several canyon systems south of the Abajo Mountains.

About a mile from the Devils Pocket trail junction, the trail enters Devils Lane, one of the many "grabens," German for "graves," in this area of the park. These long valleys roughly parallel the Colorado River gorge and were formed by the slow flow of salt deposits deep underground that produced fracturing and settling of the overlying strata. From the air, these long, narrow depressions somewhat resemble sunken graves.

In Devils Lane, the trail left is an 8-mile round trip spur that ends in Chesler Canyon at the head of the Joint Trail hiking route into Chesler Park, just beyond where it connects with the Bobbys Hole-Ruin Park trail. This connecting trail can be taken for an additional 2-1/2-mile round trip to Horsehoof Arch.

From the Devils Lane junction, the trail to the right continues the Elephant Hill loop, arriving at the head of the "Silver Stairs" in less than a mile, where the Doll House is visible to the west, in the Land of Standing Rocks.

Shortly past the Silver Stairs, the trail comes to another junction. The spur trail straight ahead is the 7-mile round-trip route to the Confluence Overlook, plus another spur up Cyclone Canyon. The spur trail to the Confluence is easy, traveling primarily on packed sediments and drift sand. The trail to the right is the 3-3/4-mile return loop back to Elephant Hill.

NOTES:

1. This trail is the last section of the Cottonwood Canyon/Beef Basin/Bobbys Hole-Ruin Park trail.

2. This trail is within Canyonlands National Park. Please keep bikes on the trails and in designated camping areas.

3. The head of this trail is also the starting point of a one-day hike up Elephant Canyon to Druid Arch. A spur of that trail goes through Chesler Park to the Joint Trail.

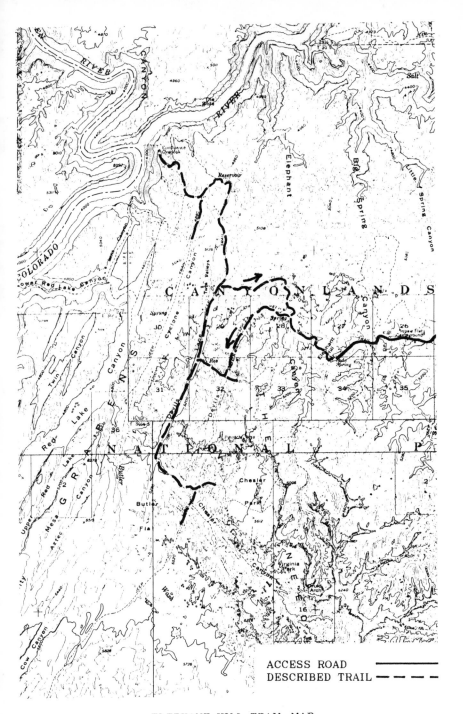

ACCESS ROAD   —————
DESCRIBED TRAIL   — — — —

ELEPHANT HILL TRAIL MAP

OTHER TRAILS

INTRODUCTION

The trails described in detail in the previous chapter were selections made by the authors based on careful consideration of all the factors involved in canyon country mountain biking. There are also dozens of other named and mapped trails in all six areas that can be traveled by mountain bikers. Some will be of little value except as connecting routes between more interesting trail segments, while others will closely rival the described trails in many ways.

The charts on the following pages list the other named trails in the region covered by this book, with certain basic data of interest to bikers listed for each, together with sources for more detailed information. How these other trails rate as bike routes will vary among individual bikers, with their different skills, preferences, tastes and interests.

In addition to the named and mapped trails in canyon country, there are hundreds of branching 4-wheeled vehicle trails and tracks that curious bikers might -- or might not -- want to explore. The only routes more aimless and unpredictable to follow than the legendary "path of the calf" are the numerous trails and tracks left by the several waves of prospectors who have periodically invaded the region.

Over the last two decades, the authors have explored hundreds of these trails-to-nowhere. Since most of them were found wanting for general recreational use, they have not been documented or mapped. Even so, tastes vary, so some bikers will no doubt find many of these unmapped trails of interest for one reason or another. Their endless numbers add to the variety and scope of canyon country mountain-biking opportunities.

MORE SLICKROCK BIKING

Once you have tried Moab's famous Slickrock Bike Trail, perhaps you would like to sample another version of slickrock biking that is even more challenging, exciting and spectacular -- and breathtaking in more ways than one.

There are any number of places in canyon country where various kinds of sandstone slickrock erode into vast expanses of rolling "petrified dunes" and "fins." The Slickrock Bike Trail provides a marked and designated area where petrified dune-biking can be sampled. There are many other similar areas, such as high atop Poison Spider Mesa or along lofty Gold Bar Rim, where freelance petrified dune-biking is practical.

There are also a very few areas where another kind of sandstone has eroded into long, terraced slopes, rather than petrified dunes or sheer cliffs. Terraced-slope slickrock routes offer a completely different kind of biking, one with no designated routes, one even more demanding and rewarding than slickrock dune-biking.

This novel kind of biking requires that the bike now and then be lifted up or down a few feet in order to attain a higher or lower terrace, or walked through an occasional rock slide, but otherwise travels winding, ascending terraces of solid, red-and-white-banded slickrock, for mile after mile, often attaining heights of hundreds of feet above canyon floors.

Terraced-slope slickrock biking is not for beginners or the faint-hearted, but in compensation offers unique challenges and opportunities. And, because of the nature of the rock, there is no limit to the number of routes that can be found and traveled, even on the same miles-long stretch of slickrock.

Canyon Country Publications is preparing a guidebook titled *Canyon Country* SLICKROCK BIKING & HIKING, but in the meantime, here are some sample routes for advanced bikers who might wish to try this unique experience.

For access to the listed routes, use the map and ORV-trail guide book for the Island Area.

Drive or bike into the lower end of Tusher Canyon to where the red-hued slickrock begins rising out of the ground. Bike up onto the lower terraces of rock on either side of the canyon and continue as far as possible. The eastern slope can be traveled all the way to an elevated summit formed by a gap between Tusher and Mill canyons, with spectacular views of the two redrock canyons, a stand of towering spires, and the Monitor and Merrimac buttes to the south. There are endless interesting and challenging biking routes on the broad summit point.

Drive to the narrow lower end of nearby Bartlett Wash and park where its slickrock walls first appear, just south of a gigantic east-west fault-line. The western slickrock slope can be traveled up onto a distant elevated point, then around that point and along the high walls of maze-like Hidden Canyon. The eastern slope can be traveled for several miles, ascending all the way, to a lofty, narrow gap between Bartlett Wash and the upper end of adjacent Tusher Canyon, for a magnificent view of both redrock canyons. With care and effort, it is possible to go beyond this gap.

Mountain bikers should sample the slickrock slopes in this area soon. Although it is presently federal land -- public land open to everyone -- it may not remain open for long. The State of Utah is attempting to acquire this unique area from the Bureau of Land Management in order to turn it over to a mining company for the creation of massive solar evaporation salt ponds, similar to those visible below Dead Horse Point State Park and along the Potash Trail. If this occurs, the entire area will be closed off as private land, off-limits for recreational use.

Bikers should take note that slickrock biking is prohibited within national and state parks and monuments, where all wheeled vehicles are required to stay on designated "jeep trails."

Tom Kuehne photo

OTHER TRAILS BY AREA

NOTES: 1. Trail lengths on spur trails are given for round trips.
2. Trail lengths on connecting and loop trails are one-way.

ARCHES AREA

BOOK: *Canyon Country* OFF-ROAD VEHICLE TRAILS, Arches & La Sals Areas.
MAP: *Canyon Country* OFF-ROAD VEHICLE TRAIL MAP, Arches & La Sals Areas.

TRAIL NAME	TYPE	LENGTH	COMMENTS
Dome Plateau	spur	35 miles	long trail, some sand, panoramas
Dry Mesa	loop	18 miles	steep access, considerable sand
Eye-of-the Whale	connecting	13 miles	scenic, but lots of sand, rough
Lost Spring Canyon	spur	9 miles	remote, scenic, lots of slickrock
Salt Valley	connecting	17 miles	dusty, little to offer bikers
Squaw Park	spur	8 miles	scenic, but easy to get lost
Willow Spring	connecting	8 miles	sandy, scenic in the park segment
Wintercamp Ridge	spur	8 miles	sandy, view of Arches from east
Yellowcat	connecting	40 miles	traverses abandoned mining area

----

CANYON RIMS AREA

BOOK: *Canyon Country* OFF-ROAD VEHICLE TRAILS, Canyon Rims & Needles Areas.
MAP: *Canyon Country* OFF-ROAD VEHICLE TRAIL MAP, Canyon Rims & Needles Areas.

TRAIL NAME	TYPE	LENGTH	COMMENTS
Cane Creek Canyon	loop	13 miles	spectacular, but sandy in main canyon
Harts Point	spur	34 miles	spectacular canyon-rim views
Hatch Point	spur	17 miles	rim views, sandy, easy to get lost
Jackson Hole	spur	12 miles	interesting erosional landforms
Lockhart Basin	connecting	40 miles	long, but spectacular redrock scenery
Looking Glass Rock	connecting	18 miles	interesting erosional landforms

----

ISLAND AREA

BOOK: *Canyon Country* OFF-ROAD VEHICLE TRAILS, Island Area.
MAP: *Canyon Country* OFF-ROAD VEHICLE TRAIL MAP, Island Area.

TRAIL NAME	TYPE	LENGTH	COMMENTS
Bartlett Rim	loop	6 miles	spectacular view of Hidden Canyon
Bartlett Wash	connecting	7-1/2 miles	scenic but sandy in places
Bull Canyon	spur	7 miles	goes below Gemini Bridges
Crystal Geyser	connecting	14-1/2 miles	cold-water geyser, river views
Four Arches	spur	4 miles	four large arches, lovely canyon
Freckle Flat	connecting	4-1/2 miles	sandy, rocky connecting route
Gold Bar Rim	spur	5 miles	slickrock, spectacular views
Hellroaring Canyon	spur	18 miles	wild canyon, but rough, eroded
Levi Well	connecting	7 miles	artesian well, but very sandy
Little Canyon	connecting	3 miles	scenic connecting trail
Long Canyon	connecting	7 miles	scenic, upper end steep and rough
Mineral Point	spur	27 miles	view of Green River, end of trail
Rainbow Rocks	connecting	6-1/2 miles	sandy, but curious erosional forms
Red Wash	connecting	6 miles	colorful, scenic, but some sand
Salt Wash	connecting	9 miles	colorful, river view, but sandy
Spring Canyon	spur	55 miles	travels in Green River gorge
Spring Canyon Point	spur	25 miles	very scenic, spectacular views
Taylor Canyon Rim	spur	15 miles	views of spectacular Taylor Canyon
Tenmile Point	spur	14 miles	sandy, remote canyon overlooks
Tenmile Wash	connecting	2-1/2 miles	old line cabin, dripping springs
White Wash	spur	optional	sand dune and slickrock recreation

LA SALS AREA

BOOK: *Canyon Country* OFF-ROAD VEHICLE TRAILS, Arches & La Sals Areas.
MAP: *Canyon Country* OFF-ROAD VEHICLE TRAIL MAP, Arches & La Sals Areas.

TRAIL NAME	TYPE	LENGTH	COMMENTS
Adobe Mesa	spur	12 miles	spectacular views of river gorge
Beaver Basin	spur	10 miles	high mountain basin, old mines
Cottonwood Canyon	connecting	7 miles	steep, rough, spectacular views
Dark Canyon	connecting	12 miles	rough in places, mountain lake
Dolores River	spur	26 miles	historic cabins, scenic gorge
Dolores River Overlook	spur	11 miles	river gorge views, side trails
La Sal Pass	connecting	15 miles	very steep, summit may be closed
Miners Basin	spur	8 miles	high basin, old mining settlement
Oowah Lake	spur	7 miles	mountain lake, stream, camping
Powerpole Rim	spur	9 miles	fine view, but steep and rough
Sand Flats	connecting	19 miles	very scenic, take downhill direction
Top-of-the-World	spur	10 miles	spectacular view, but steep, rough

MAZE AREA

BOOK: *Canyon Country* OFF-ROAD VEHICLE TRAILS, Maze Area.
MAP: *Canyon Country* OFF-ROAD VEHICLE TRAIL MAP, Maze Area.

TRAIL NAME	TYPE	LENGTH	COMMENTS
Anderson Bottom	spur	44 miles	long, rough, but scenic trail
Big Ridge	spur	26 miles	lofty, spectacular overlooks
Horseshoe Canyon	spur	36 miles	prehistoric rock art sites
Maze Overlook	spur	28 miles	outstanding views of The Maze
Panorama Point	spur	16 miles	high point overlooking The Maze
Queen Anns Bottom	spur	6 miles	spur beyond Anderson Bottom
Sunset Pass	spur	4 miles	to pass summit viewpoint only
The Spur	spur	26 miles	spectacular Green River gorge

NEEDLES AREA

BOOK: *Canyon Country* OFF-ROAD VEHICLE TRAILS, Canyon Rims & Needles Areas.
MAP: *Canyon Country* OFF-ROAD VEHICLE TRAIL MAP, Canyon Rims & Needles Areas.

TRAIL NAME	TYPE	LENGTH	COMMENTS
Big Pocket Overlook	spur	5 miles	outstanding view, upper Salt Creek
Davis Canyon	spur	20 miles	arches, ruins, but very sandy
Horse Canyon	spur	15 miles	arches, ruins, but very sandy
Lavender Canyon	spur	26 miles	arches, ruins, scenic, but sandy
Salt Creek Canyon	spur	30 miles	Angel Arch, ruins, but very sandy

Tom Kuehne photo

FAVORITE TRAILS

Following is a list of ten trails favored by mountain bikers who have already sampled some of what canyon country has to offer. As the region and its trails become better known to bikers, other trails may replace some of these as overall favorites, but this list will at least give bikers new to canyon country a menu of trails to sample that have already proven to be popular.

1. Cane Creek Canyon Rim/Pritchett Canyon Trail
2. Cottonwood Canyon/Beef Basin/Bobbys Hole-Ruin Park Trail
3. Shafer/Potash Trail
4. Gemini Bridges Trail
5. White Rim Trail
6. Colorado River Overlook Trail
7. Poison Spider Mesa Trail
8. Monitor & Merrimac Trail
9. Hurrah Pass/Chicken Corners Trail
10. Hidden Canyon Rim Trail

SPECIAL EVENTS

The Moab Fat Tire Festival has become perhaps the best-known mountain bike event in the country. It consists of a week, in late October, of guided group rides, hill climbs, time trials, slide shows and presentations on such diverse subjects as archaeology, climbing, desert biking and desert ecology. The event usually ends with a Halloween costume bash.

A brochure, printed annually, is available from local bike shops and the Moab visitor center. The town enjoys a carnival atmosphere during this week. Advance registration is desirable.

Other annual events in Moab are the Moab Stage Race, the Half-Marathon, and the Easter Jeep Safari.

The Moab Stage Race is a two-day road-racing event for bikes. From 1985 through 1987, it used a route partly in Arches National Park, but may use a different route in the future.

The annual Moab Half-Marathon is a major springtime event, drawing more than a thousand runners a year. The event consists of a half-marathon and a five-mile run along a magnificent road in the bottom of the red-walled Colorado River gorge.

The Easter Jeep Safari is not a biking event, but is as popular and well-known to ORV fans as the Fat Tire Festival is to ATB aficionados. It draws participants from far and wide in Easter week. The carnival atmosphere and crowds exceed even those of the Fat Tire Festival. Bikers need not avoid Moab then, but should be aware of the event, and of the likelihood of encountering ORV convoys on many of the trails, especially in the Island and Canyon Rims areas. The event is sponsored and organized by the Red Rock 4-Wheelers, a Moab ORV club.

Information about biking and other events is available at Moab bike shops and the Moab Visitor Center, 805 North Main Street (U.S.191), Moab, Utah 84532. Telephone (801) 259-8825.

ACKNOWLEDGMENTS

I wish to express my thanks to all the many individuals, organizations and businesses who aided me while I gathered information for this book. The names of some are listed below. Others were very helpful even though anonymous.

For example, I solicited input with a formal survey of one hundred bikers during the Fat Tire Festival of 1987. Their names were not recorded, but their opinions, preferences and interests were used as guidelines for the selection of material to put in this book. My sincere thanks to these individuals, and to the many bikers I encountered and interviewed on the trails.

I am also indebted to several businesses, and their representatives, for their consideration and technical assistance. These are:

James Fox and Shane King, Red Rock Bike Shoppe & Shuttles, Moab, Utah,

Ken Talor, Rainbow Cycles, Midvale, Utah, and

Bert Fox, Cycles Peugeot USA, West Point, Utah.

Representatives of the three regional land administration agencies provided technical expertise and encouragement. My special thanks to:

Thea Nordling of the National Park Service,

Pat Spahr of the U. S. Forest Service, and

Russ Von Koch of the Bureau of Land Management.

My gratitude also to:

Barney and Jean Phelps, for trails information,

Bego, for technical climbing information,

Terby Barnes, for cheerful typing and proof-reading,

Christine Beckman, Rodney Taylor, Dan Sims and Glen Lathrop, for trail-riding, biking insights, and camaraderie,

Mark and Chris Davis of the Needles Outpost, for knowing and loving the land, and hospitably being there,

Eric Bajon, for technical outdoors guidance, insistence on accuracy of description, and infectious enthusiasm, and

Linda Kuehne, my wife, for riding trails, taking photographs, and being a kind critic and best friend.

If I have failed to acknowledge someone who was helpful with this project it was unintentional, and I hereby extend blanket gratitude to everyone, whether or not named above.

Tom Kuehne

FURTHER READING

Mountain bikers who wish to know more about the unique and fascinating canyon country of southeastern Utah will find other books and maps in the *Canyon Country* series both useful and informative. They are stocked by many visitor centers and retail outlets in the region, or can be ordered through book stores.

The listed books are profusely illustrated with photographs, charts, graphs, maps and original artwork. The maps are also illustrated with representative photographs.

GENERAL INFORMATION

Canyon Country HIGHWAY TOURING by F. A. Barnes. A guide to the highways and roads in the region that can safely be traveled by highway vehicles, plus descriptions of all the national and state parks and monuments and other special areas in the region.

Canyon Country EXPLORING by F. A. Barnes. A brief history of early explorations, plus details concerning the administration of this vast area of public land and exploring the region today by land, air and water.

Canyon Country CAMPING by F. A. Barnes. A complete guide to all kinds of camping in the region, including highway pull-offs, developed public and commercial campgrounds, and backcountry camping from vehicles and backpacks.

Canyon Country GEOLOGY by F. A. Barnes. A summary of the unique geologic history of the region for the general reader, with a list of its unusual land-forms and a section on rock collecting.

Canyon Country PREHISTORIC INDIANS by Barnes & Pendleton. A detailed description of the region's two major prehistoric Indian cultures, with sections telling where to view their ruins, rock art and artifacts.

Canyon Country PREHISTORIC ROCK ART by F. A. Barnes. A comprehensive study of the mysterious prehistoric rock art found throughout the region, with a section listing places where it can be viewed.

Canyon Country ARCHES & BRIDGES by F. A. Barnes. A complete description of the unique natural arches, bridges and windows found throughout the region, with hundreds depicted.

UTAH CANYON COUNTRY by F. A. Barnes. An overview of the entire region's natural and human history, parks and monuments, and recreational opportunities, illustrated in full color.

CANYONLANDS NATIONAL PARK - Early History & First Descriptions by F. A. Barnes. A summary of the early history of this uniquely spectacular national park, including quotes from the journals of the first explorers to see and describe it.